Endorsements for *Life Changing Encounters and Divine Appointments*

Romans 8:28 tells us that everything happens for a reason. There are no accidents or happenstance. In **Life-Changing Encounters and Divine Appointments***, Sue Z. McGray demonstrates how God can take everyday encounters and use them for life-changing impact. Through twenty-five Bible examples as well as personal examples from her own life, she reminds us that God is always at work in our lives in ways we may never fully appreciate until we look back and see how He led us through those seemingly ordinary encounters and used them to deliver us to divine appointments.*

·Sharon Wilharm
; Women podcast
icated radio show

You will be blessed in reading the book that you hold in your hands. As you journey with Sue McGray through twenty-five divine encounters of God's Word, you will also learn much about how God touched her life through many similar "divine encounters."

I know Sue McGray, and her husband Duane, to be good and godly people who serve the Lord with gladness. Sue is a very successful businesswoman. Duane retired from a career in law enforcement. Both experienced the hand of God in their lives. It was, no doubt, a divine encounter that led them to each other. Sue has experienced the hand of God, the protection of

God, and the direction of God in her life through all of those experiences, God has granted her wisdom. You will find that her wisdom is captured in the "Life Application" section of each chapter.

This book will be a blessing in your life.

-**Bruce G. Chesser, Senior Pastor**
First Baptist Church
Hendersonville, Tennessee

Life-Changing Encounters and Divine Appointments is a must-read for anyone who has a desire to understand how personal encounters can change their life. Sue Z McGray recounts the stories of people whose lives have been altered by their own personal encounters. More importantly, the author reveals many "life-altering" encounters experienced by biblical characters and what we can learn from them. Their stories emphasize the truths of the Bible with fresh insights concerning how their personal encounters can shape our lives and guide our behavior. Understanding these encounters can change the destiny of readers as they better understand the relevance of these biblical encounters.

-**James C Hutchins, D. MIN.**
Retired Academic Dean
Covington Theological Seminary

This marvelous book by Sue Z McGray is a fresh look at the transformational power of divine, life-altering encounters *experienced by some of our most well-known and beloved Bible characters in the Old and New Testaments, as well as the author's own life. Each engaging, bite-sized chapter delivers giant spiritual insights and reminders of God's redeeming work in our lives to help us find our true purpose and become fruitful ambassadors for the Kingdom. The thought-provoking questions at the end of each section make the book ideal for personal as well as small group studies. This is a most enjoyable and edifying read for seekers at all stages of their spiritual journey.*

-Marion M. Pyle, M.A.
Television Writer, Director,
Producer and Host, Legacy Media Lab, Inc.
Author and speaker,
Healed, Healthy and Whole, How We Beat Cancer.

*Sue has a unique ability to relate to people in whatever life situation they are in. Her book, **Life-Changing Encounters and Divine Appointments**, is her latest effort to share this ability and she has succeeded wonderfully. Reading this book will be a joy and blessing to all and one you will want to share with others. God has used Sue in many ways and her book is an expression of His love for each of us and her.*

-Lynn Starks

Sue's book is such a great reminder of God's love and faithfulness! I love how she combined Bible stories from long ago and her own personal experiences to help us notice our own divine appointments; our life-altering encounters. It was refreshing and encouraging to remember God's engagement in our lives—in the small moments and in those more life-changing moments. Sue's desire and commitment to living a life of faithfulness and obedience and love shines through her words. They have prompted me to watch for more of my own divine appointments.

-Gaye Lindfors, Speaker, Blogger, and Author of *Getting My Ducks in a Row and Other Stories of Faith.*

Wow! What can I say about **Life-Changing Encounters and Divine Appointments?** This book is a wonderful reminder of how God moves. Believe me if you are looking to be reminded of God's goodness and His word, pick up this book and read it NOW. It's time to be renewed and refreshed.

-Lisa Hooks, M.A.
Purpose Bourn Coaching

It is one thing to believe in God. It's quite another thing to believe in a God who chooses to reveal Himself to His creation in very real and personal ways. Sue McGray's book, **Life-Changing Encounters and Divine Appointments**, is an extreme faith builder that underscores how God goes out of His way to make Himself known to anyone who will dare to believe.

-Monica Schmelter
Host, Bridges
- daily television show that airs

in over **50 million homes**
on Christian Television Network
<u>ctntv.org</u>

Because of her engaging style, I read Sue McGray's last book in one sitting and this new offering is no different. Sue reminds us that our divine encounters can change the direction of our lives, even as they did in the lives of the biblical leaders. God still connects His people in supernatural ways that we cannot deny. This book is a must-read!

-Lisa Burkhardt Worley
Author, Speaker, POP Talk Executive
Producer/Co-Host Pearls of Promise Ministries
<u>www.pearlsofpromiseministries.com</u>
Facebook: /pearlsofpromiseministries/
Twitter: @pearlsofpromise
Instagram: @popministries

LIFE CHANGING ENCOUNTERS
AND
Divine
APPOINTMENTS

Twenty-Five Biblical Encounters That Provide Insight
for Personal Encounters in the 21st Century.

God actively fulfills His purposes through spirit-led encounters between believers and seekers.

SUE Z MCGRAY

XULON PRESS

Xulon Press
2301 Lucien Way #415
Maitland, FL 32751
407.339.4217
www.xulonpress.com

Library of Congress Control Number: 2021921163

Paperback ISBN-13: 978-1-6628-3375-5
Ebook ISBN-13: 978-1-6628-3376-2

Table of Contents

Acknowledgements

I want to thank my dear friends, Lynn Starks, Dr. Phil Lily, his wife Carol, Diane Burton, and my husband Duane for their insight and assistance in the writing of this book, and Steve Heim for his challenging belief in the importance of encounters. Their help was invaluable. I expressly want to acknowledge the Holy Spirit for inspiring me to write this book and for providing spiritual guidance.

Preface

God gives us encounters as opportunities to grow spiritually and to add value to the lives of other people. He often creates divine appointments for us to fulfil a mission. As you read each chapter, let God inspire you to use your own encounters in a way that will enrich your spiritual life and challenge you to better understand the importance of encounters in your own life, and that of others. I have shared some life-altering encounters and divine appointments that have impacted my life and which I hope help you in your journey. My prayer is that as you read the pages of this book, that you will recall moments in your life that were life-changing, even divine appointments.

As a young woman and a new mom, I had an encounter that changed the course of my life. I was checking groceries at our local grocery when a lady came through my line and mentioned something about me trying a new eye shadow.

Her skin was beautiful, and I thought, I would love to have beautiful skin too. I knew I could not afford a new eye shadow, but I remember thinking, *When I can afford it, I want to use what she had on her face.* I never got to know this lady, but she planted a seed that would lead me to a career I loved. I knew nothing about cosmetics, nor anything about being an entrepreneur and running a business. The thought of being in sales was not something I was comfortable with. Because of this encounter with a stranger and a moment in time, I embarked on a thirty-seven-year career in the cosmetics business.

The cosmetics business gave me an opportunity to grow. Our founder, Mary Kay Ash, was a Christian who taught things like practicing the Golden Rule, and having a go give spirit. The life lessons I learned from her had nothing to do with cosmetics but rather living a more positive, Christ-filled life. Beyond learning about cosmetics and running a business, I learned to develop a belief in myself that had never existed before. I loved every moment of my career. Many of the people in my life today are because of the encounter with an unnamed lady at a grocery store. At the time of that encounter, I did not realize how it would forever change me.

I have also experienced what I honestly believe were divine appointments. During a period of intense personal turmoil, as my marriage was falling apart, I had an encounter with my friend, Patty, who challenged my faith. It turned out to be a wake-up call that forced me to think and act differently. Then there was an encounter with a man who would become my husband and soulmate. Looking back on these encounters, I believe they were divine appointments.

We all have stories of encounters that have altered our lives. What can seem to be inconsequential meetings between people often have a significant impact. Some simply cannot be explained other than the encounter was divinely orchestrated. Many stories found in the Bible are of encounters that altered biblical and world history. Each chapter of this book contains a section that describes a biblical encounter and another section that discusses a life application of what can be learned from this encounter. These are stories that retain their relevance today. They are spiritually inspiring and teach us to seek God's plan for the next stage of our lives. Ask yourself: How does this encounter affect me?

Remember, encounters really do matter. It is up to us to make the most of what we learn from the encounters described in the Bible and in our own lives to grasp the importance of taking all encounters seriously.

May God grant you fresh new encounters (divine appointments) each day that will positively impact your life and others.

Introduction

It was late in the afternoon when the disciple Cleopas and a friend were walking along the long, dusty road from Jerusalem to the small village of Emmaus. Toward the end of their nineteen-mile walk, they suddenly found themselves in the company of a fellow traveler, a stranger. The stranger listened in as they recounted the crucifixion and death of Jesus of Nazareth. The stranger could tell that the two disciples of the Christ were troubled and "downcast." In so many words, the stranger asked Cleopas and his friend, "What are these words that you are exchanging with one another as you are walking?" The two travelers were astounded that the stranger had no knowledge of the events that had just occurred three days previous in Jerusalem. Because their eyes had "prevented them," they were unaware the stranger in their company was indeed Jesus the Christ. During the remaining portion of their journey and at dinner that evening, Jesus reintroduced them and others to the Gospel. Then during supper, as Jesus "broke bread and blessed it," their eyes were opened, and they recognized Him. Can you even imagine their astonishment and wonder..the risen Christ was in their presence? What an encounter!

This is just one of many encounters God orchestrated in the Old and New Testament Eras. Since man began populating the earth, people have been encountering others. Encounters can be planned, accidental, with purpose, meaningful, harmful, or casual. Each day, we all have encounters that have the potential of altering the direction of our lives or of someone else. Come now and read along as Sue Z. McGray recounts twenty-five of the most poignant encounters in Scripture. Once considered and applied to your day-to-day life, encounters will take on a totally different meaning and a lasting impact. God's blessings to the reader.

Rev. Dr. Philip G. Lilly

1

Saul's Blinding Encounter

Saul's Encounter with Jesus on the Damascus Road

Acts 9

Throughout history there have been billions of encounters between people that have altered their life and the lives of others. Most of those encounters matter little to anyone other than the people directly involved. Other encounters leave a deep and lasting impact on many people. It has been said there is a reason for every meeting we have. Encounters that are orchestrated by God are vital to His work on earth. One of the most impactful encounters in human history is the encounter that Saul had with Jesus as he journeyed on the road to Damascus.

The Encounter

The story of Saul's encounter with Jesus is found in chapter 9 of the Book of Acts. When Saul encountered Jesus on the road to Damascus, all of mankind was impacted. The encounter was revolutionary as it opened a pathway for the gospel to spread around the whole world. Acts paints a vibrant picture of the early Christian church and the spread of the gospel. The Apostle Peter preached primarily to Jewish people and Saul, after his encounter with Jesus, spread the good news to the Gentile world. Saul of Tarsus became Paul the Apostle as the result of his remarkable and divine encounter with Jesus.

Saul was a first century Hebrew born in the city of Tarsus. His early life was characterized as being a profoundly zealous Pharisee who persecuted Christians and ended his life being martyred as a staunch believer and evangelical proponent of Christ. He received a formal religious education under the teaching of Rabbi Gamaliel, a leading first century authority of the Jewish religion. Through Gamaliel's teachings, Saul developed an in-depth understanding of Jewish history and religious law. With his training and Pharisaic influence, he

Paul the Apostle, original name Saul of Tarsus, was born in what is now Turkey—died 62–64 in Rome. He was one of the leaders of the first generation of Christians, often considered to be the most important person after Jesus in the history of Christianity.

became an ardent persecutor of early believers of Christ. He was present and fully approved of the mob's actions when Stephen was stoned to death to become the first Christian martyr. Saul ravaged the church, entering the homes of believers and committing them to prison. He had no idea that he would have an encounter (divine appointment) with Jesus, one day as he walked along the hot and dusty road on his way to Damascus on a mission to arrest and extradite Christians back to Jerusalem for trial.

As he walked, Saul experienced a blinding encounter with Jesus that resulted in him becoming an ardent missionary, taking the message of Christ to an unbelieving Gentile world. His ministry included three missionary journeys, several letters to churches that are included in the New Testament and a tremendous example of faithful service in the face of fierce persecution. His education, background as a Pharisee, Roman citizenship, and unflagging zeal contributed to his success as a missionary to the Gentile world.

> *3 As he traveled and was nearing Damascus, a light from heaven suddenly flashed around him. 4 Falling to the ground, he heard a voice saying to him, "Saul, Saul, why are you persecuting me?" 5 "Who are you, Lord?" Saul said. "I am Jesus, the one you are persecuting," he replied. 6 "But get up and go into the city, and you will be told what you must do." 7 The men who were traveling with him stood speechless,*

*hearing the sound but seeing no one. 8
Saul got up from the ground, and though
his eyes were open, he could see nothing.
So they took him by the hand and led him
into Damascus.*

Acts 9:3-8.

Following his encounter with Jesus, Saul was taken to Damascus where he remained for three days, unable to see. A disciple named Ananias was living in Damascus and God spoke to him in a vision, telling him to go to Saul and place hands on him to restore his vision. At first Ananias was reluctant to go because of Saul's reputation. But God revealed to Ananias that He had a mission for Saul. As Ananias obeyed God, he healed Saul's blindness and told him he would be filled with the Holy Spirit. Saul was immediately healed, and he was baptized, and his name was changed to Paul.

A Life Application

*Throughout the Bible
God has set apart
people for himself and to
accomplish his purposes.*

All of Paul's previous life experiences were preparing him for a life dedicated to reaching the world with the good news that had been previously limited to the Jews. That preparation was the work of God and was in ways he could not have imagined. His encounter with Jesus resulted in a complete turnaround in his lifelong beliefs and a new life.

A saving encounter with Jesus always results in a sinful past being forgiven and the start of a new life. Like Paul, our past experiences can be used by God, even when they were controlled by sin. A past involving alcoholism, sex addiction, and abuse are all experiences that can be used to help others experiencing those issues. Celebrate Recovery is a ministry that uses redeemed sufferers of addiction to help people in need of help. As a victim of domestic abuse, I have experienced things that prepared me to mentor women who are living with similar abuse. While Christians have a new life that is a radical reversal from their pasts, their past experiences can be useful tools in service to the Lord.

Some of the most powerful Christian testimonies involve a past mired in the worst kind of sin and failure. They are stories of forgiveness and transformation. In our encounters with others, we have an opportunity to share the good news with others so they might also find a new life. All Christians should ponder their own past and their personal encounter with Jesus. Everyone travels the road of life headed in their own direction. An encounter with Jesus results in a change in direction. If there is no change in direction, there cannot have been a life-altering encounter with Jesus.

One lesson from Paul's new life in Christ is that while believers have the joy of forgiveness and salvation, they are not guaranteed to live an ideal or pain-free life. Soon after Saul's encounter with Jesus, Jews conspired to kill him.

Other disciples remembered he had a history of killing Christian believers and were afraid of him. Throughout the remainder of his life, Paul was persecuted, imprisoned, and martyred because of his commitment to Jesus. Paul described his life, prior to and after his encounter with Jesus, in his letter to the church at Philippi.

> **7 I have considered to be a loss because of Christ. 8 More than that, I also consider everything to be a loss in view of the surpassing value of knowing Christ Jesus my Lord.**
>
> Philippians 3:7-8

> **10 My goal is to know him and the power of his resurrection and the fellowship of his sufferings, being conformed to his death, 11 assuming that I will somehow reach the resurrection from among the dead.**
>
> Philippians 3:10-11

Paul's commitment was the result of a divine encounter on his way to Damascus, which gave him the joy of having a relationship with Jesus and serving Him, even while suffering persecution. His letter to the church at Philippi is the most joyful book in the Bible. He uses the Greek words for joy and rejoicing numerous times while writing from a dingy Roman prison. Paul focused on joy rather than his afflictions. We should live with the same level of joy in Christ. All our encounters should be understood as potential divine appointments and an opportunity to share the good news of Jesus with others. God wants us to enter each encounter with purpose and with the expectation it may be a divine appointment orchestrated by the Holy Spirit. It is the Holy Spirit who prepares people as He works to open hearts to be ready for encounters with the gospel.

> **26 "But the Advocate, the Holy Spirit, whom the Father will send in my name, will teach you all things and will remind you of everything I have said to you."**
>
> John 14:26

Our encounters are vastly different than that of Saul on the Damascus Road, however, all Christians have their own divine encounter with Jesus as they travel the road of life. Paul's encounter was transformational, as ours should be. History remembers Paul as a prolific evangelist, not for his life as a devout Pharisee. Even Wikipedia defines Paul as a Christian apostle who spread the teachings of Jesus in the first-century world and as one of the most important figures of the Apostolic Age. He founded several Christian communities in Asia Minor and Europe from the mid-30s to the mid-50s AD. There is no better way to be remembered.

Will you be remembered for your life before becoming a believer or your new life as a disciple of Jesus? Was your life transformed when you encountered Jesus? Our encounters may not be blinding, but if they are true encounters with Jesus, they will always be transformational and life-changing. God wants us to be remembered as people who used our encounters with others to spread the gospel in our world. We all have life experiences that can be used by God. He has prepared us with a testimony, and we should use it in our encounters.

Scripture Reading

Acts 8:1-3
Acts 9:1-30

Takeaway Questions

Paul's encounter with Jesus on the Damascus Road changed his life entirely. Have you experienced an encounter with Jesus that resulted in a changed life? Take a few minutes to document how your life changed.

Have there been times when you shared with others your conversion encounter with Jesus? Explain.

What life applications from this study do you believe apply to your life as you have encounters with other people?

Notes

2

Jacob's Fearful Encounter

Jacob Lived in Fear of an Encounter with Esau

GENESIS 32

*M*any people live defeated lives, crippled with fear and anxiety, because of imagined problems that may not actually exist. That is not the kind of life God wants for us. Trust and faith in Him will provide peace and joy, not anxiety.

The Encounter

The Book of Genesis provides the story of Jacob, who feared an expected encounter with his brother Esau. The story involves both brothers as they progressed toward a reunion after twenty years of separation and estrangement. Jacob knew he had wronged his brother and had allowed himself to build up dread and fear, in his mind, of the upcoming encounter. While he feared the encounter, it was also something he had desired since their separation. Jacob prayed to God for divine help in the approaching crisis, to protect him and his family against Esau's imagined vengeance. He could not control the situation himself, so he placed the problem in God's hands.

> **11 " *Please rescue me from my brother Esau, for I am afraid of him."***
>
> Genesis 32:11

The story began in Genesis 25, when Jacob caused his brother Esau to sell him the family birthright that rightly belonged to Esau. Then in chapter 27, Jacob's mother Rebekah conspired with him to deceive his father Isaac into unwittingly giving the family blessing to him, rather than Esau, to whom it belonged. Jacob's years of fear stemmed from

The name Jacob means "supplanter" or "deceiver". An apt description for the Patriarch Jacob before his life was changed. After his night of wrestling with God, his Name was changed to Israel.

a guilty conscience arising out of the deception he used and Esau's threat to kill him.

> **41 Esau held a grudge against Jacob because of the blessing his father had given him. And Esau determined in his heart, "The days of mourning for my**

> ***father are approaching; then I will kill my***
> ***brother Jacob."***
>
> Genesis 27:41

After his deception and theft, Jacob fled to escape his brother's vengeance. Twenty years had passed since Jacob had separated from his family, and in Genesis 32, he is found preparing for a reunion encounter with Esau. One can imagine the thoughts Jacob had conjured up in his mind over those twenty years, knowing the state of their relationship and Esau's threat when they last saw one another. The longer he imagined the problem, the greater the problem grew in his mind.

Jacob prepared for his encounter with Esau by sending messengers ahead to meet him. The messengers were told to tell Esau of his hope that he had favor in his brother's eyes. When they returned, they told him, "Esau is coming to meet you with four hundred men." The news added to Jacob's fear and distress.

Then Jacob did the right thing: he prayed to God to save him. During the night, he experienced another encounter, this time with an angel who wrestled with him until morning. His dream was a divine encounter that resulted in Jacob's name being changed to Israel. This was his third encounter with God during his journey (Gen. 27:12-15, Gen. 31:10-16).

When the long-anticipated encounter finally took place, Jacob's fears melted away when his brother Esau ran to meet him and embraced him; he threw his arms around his neck and kissed him. At that point, Jacob's fears turned into tears of joy. God intervened in the encounter because he had prayerfully requested His help. The situation needed divine intervention.

A Life Application

Human interactions often turn into broken relationships. That can be especially painful when it happens among family members. My husband had two uncles who were estranged brothers who did not speak to one another for many years. When one brother died, the other brother was so vengeful that he refused to attend the funeral. Sadly, they probably did not recall what caused the split in the first place.

Jacob had clearly wronged his brother. His actions resulted in two decades of personal guilt, remorse, fear, and a loss of relationship. These had to be haunting emotions. What a burden that must have been. The internal torture Jacob experienced tore into his soul but had no impact on Esau. That is how it almost always works. When people hold a grudge against one another or harbor unconfessed guilt for their actions toward others, they are the ones affected. The other person usually goes through life unaffected and unaware.

I recently watched a movie about a young man who was in love with a girl but became emotionally devastated when she told him she was in love with his best friend. For the next seven years, he allowed himself to live a life dominated with pain and hate. His hate for his former best friend and girlfriend undermined how he related to everyone he encountered. The result was a sad period of bitterness. In the last part of the movie there was the long-hoped-for happy ending when he allowed God to heal his wounds and open his heart to forgiveness. Unfortunately, the reunion took place as he visited his friend who was on his deathbed. Years of friendship had been squandered. When he mended fences with his friend, he was healed from all the negative influences that had impacted his relationships. Later he married another girl, and I suppose lived happily ever after. His restored broken relationship with his friend could not repair seven years of pain and damaged encounters with many other people. That damage could not be erased. They are wasted years. It is unhealthy to carry negative baggage throughout life and allow it to undermine relationships with others, and more importantly, with our Lord.

Jacob desperately wanted a reunion encounter with his brother but lived in fear of it. His fear was based on perception rather than reality. We all are wired with emotions like guilt, fear, and hate. Unfortunately, we sometimes allow those emotions to override the better emotion of love.

Some of the things we want the most are the very things we fear the most. Jacob prepared for his encounter with Esau but, more importantly, he prayed to God for help during his time of distress. That is a life application example for us. We should seek God's direction when we prepare for potentially uncomfortable encounters. Because He gives us the right words at the right time, we can speak in confidence. God has given us the Holy Spirit who is with us, guiding and helping us to encounter others without fear.

Not all encounters are comfortable, but they still can be productive if we allow the Holy Spirit to guide our steps and words. When we pray for God's assistance, He goes ahead of us, preparing the way just as He did with Esau. Rather than turning the encounter into an armed conflict, Jacob's reunion with Esau was one of joy.

We do not have to live our lives the way Jacob did. Guilt and anxiety produce stress that can easily be replaced with peace and tranquility as we make things right with others and especially with God. The longer we go without confronting our fears, the greater those fears are magnified in our minds. Fear and chronic anxiety can interfere with the quality of life and can have serious consequences on physical, emotional, and spiritual health. Spiritually, fear and anxiety interfere with our relationship with God as they are an indication of lack of faith and trust in Him. This also impacts how we relate to others. When our joy in Christ is undermined, it is reflected in all aspects of our lives. Our goal should be to live victorious lives in the power of Christ as we place our faith and trust in Him.

Jacob finally did the right thing: he prayed and asked God to rescue him. He admitted his fears and placed his trust in God for protection. By doing so, he ended twenty years of anxiety and provided a valuable lesson for all of us.

Scripture Reading

Genesis 25:19 -Genesis 28:6
Genesis 32:1-Genesis 33:17

Takeaway Questions

Many times, our fears are overblown because of the anxiety we place on ourselves that is not based on fact. This story shows how Jacob conjured up a fear in his mind of something that proved to be untrue. Have you ever experienced times in your life that you allowed fear and anxiety to control you, only to learn that fear was not based on fact? Explain.

How did Jacob's unsubstantiated fear control his preparation for his encounter with his brother?

How do you think the encounter between Jacob and Esau changed their relationship? Can you think of a broken relationship of your own that perhaps is based on preconceived ideas that might not be factual? What can you do to mend that relationship?

Notes

_____

_____

_____

_____

_____

_____

_____

_____

_____

_____

_____

_____

_____

_____

_____

_____

3

David's Encounter with a Giant

David's Encounter with the Philistine Giant Goliath

1 SAMUEL 17

*L*ife comes with problems that can have giant proportions. They can be financial, loss of relationships, temptation to sin, or a myriad of other challenges. How we deal with our encounters with giants can be influenced by our faith. In 1 Samuel chapter 17, there is a story of a teenage shepherd boy who encountered a giant warrior in battle and won a tremendous victory.

Giant problems can seem impossible to overcome but when we look at them from God's perspective, we realize that God will fight for us and with us. No giants are too big for God.

The Encounter

Stories about challenging encounters do not get any better than David and Goliath. David was a shepherd boy who had an encounter with a giant Philistine warrior. The story provides an example of relying on God for victory.

The Philistines were a constant enemy of Israel. Their conflict was over land and vastly different cultures. The battle took place in approximately 1066 BC.

The Philistine army was prepared for battle and was camped facing King Saul and the Israelites. The Philistines occupied one hill and the Israelites another, with a valley between them. They were led by a giant of a man named Goliath who stood over nine feet tall and was fully armored. He continually shouted intimidating taunts to the Israelites. His taunts terrified them. David traveled back and forth between his flocks and the battle front to check on his brothers, who were serving with Saul's army. He heard the taunts and observed the Israelites flee in fear each time they saw and heard Goliath.

> *8 He stood and shouted to the Israelite battle formations: "Why do you come out to line up in battle formation?" He asked them, "Am I not a Philistine and are you not servants of Saul? Choose one of your men and have him come down against me. 9 If he wins in a fight against me and kills me, we will be your servants. But if I win against him and kill him, then you will be our servants and serve*

us." 10 Then the Philistine said, "I defy the
ranks of Israel today. Send me a man so we
can fight each other!" 11 When Saul and all
Israel heard these words from the Philistine,
they lost their courage and were terrified.

1 Samuel 17: 8-11

David made it known he would fight the giant, so Saul sent for him. He told the king not to be discouraged, that he would go and fight this Philistine. Saul told David he could not face the giant warrior as he was just a youth. David, however, knew the Lord had rescued him from wild animals and had faith that God would rescue him from the giant. Saul believed David's decision to be folly, but he still dressed him in armor. David told him he could not wear the armor because he was not accustomed to wearing it.

David's faith in God was so great that he boldly ran toward his encounter with the giant, rather than fearfully retreating from it as his fellow Israelites were in the habit of doing. As he approached the giant, Goliath looked him over and saw that he was a mere boy and taunted him even more. David's response was a testimony of his faith and trust in God who was his sustainer.

45 "You come against me with sword and
spear and javelin, but I come against you
in the name of the Lord Almighty."

1 Samuel 17:45

David slung a stone from his slingshot at Goliath and it struck him on the forehead, which killed him. When the Philistines saw their hero was dead, it was their turn to be in fear. The Philistines did what so many people do. They placed their trust in a man rather than the almighty God.

A Life Application

Christian film maker Alex Kendrick has produced a faith-based movie entitled, *Facing the Giants*, that was inspired by David's epic encounter with the Philistine giant. The film has been viewed by millions of people, which serves as a reminder that biblical encounters continue to resonate centuries later. It is a story of a Christian high school football coach who used his undying faith to battle his personal giants of fear and failure. He had never led his team to a winning season, and he faced several devastating circumstances in his personal life. In desperation he cried out to God. He received a message from an unexpected visitor that led him to search for a greater purpose for his football team. He challenged his players to believe God for the impossible, both on and off the field. When faced with unbelievable odds, the team needed to step up to their greatest test with strength and courage. What transpired is a dramatic story of struggle in which faith overcame fear. The team overcame the odds throughout the season and played a powerful team named (of course) the Giants in the state championship game and came out victorious. In the locker room, the coach asked his players to dare tell him what they believed was impossible with God. The answer, of course, was "Nothing." The team faced their fears with God's help.

Each of us have encounters with giants in one form or another. The greatest giant we face is spiritual and demonic. David faced a giant he could see; we face unseen giants. Satan is at war with mankind, and while we can see the outcome of his destruction, he works in ways that make it impossible for us to see the damage until it is too late. David did not need Saul's armor to face his giant. Our struggle is not against flesh and blood, but against cosmic powers of darkness, evil, and spiritual forces. Because of the spiritual nature of the spiritual giants we encounter, God has provided us with armor. We must put on the full armor of God so we can stand against the schemes of the devil.

Giants come in many forms, they can be family problems, work issues, friendship challenges, temptation to sin, etc. No matter what encounters you face with giants remember David's source of strength is still available to us today.

David had no fear as he encountered the giant. His strength to overcome fear came from his unwavering assurance that God, who created the universe, would sustain him. We have access to the same assurance that upheld David. Like David, we do not have to fear or waver when faced with giants in our lives. When others cowered in fear, David ran directly toward his encounter with Goliath because he had faith and trust in God. His brothers and many others had a low opinion of David, but that did not matter to him, he only cared about God's opinion of him.

The giants of life can be problems, pressures, pains, and persecutions that everyone experiences. Giants can cause major difficulties for us. It is important to realize that a giant is anything that takes our focus off God. When we overcome the giants in our lives, we can experience the love and joy in our relationship with the Father. The challenge for believers is to enter every encounter, good or bad, with faith and assurance that God will sustain us. David looked to his past and remembered that God had rescued him from wild animals. That gave him courage to place his trust in God when facing the giant. God has preserved each of us in the past and we have that experience to draw on as we face the giants in our lives. Is your faith sufficient to face any giant you encounter? Do you care more about God's opinion of you or the opinions of your peers? Peer approval is a giant that challenges most people. It can come from co-workers, friends, loved ones, or a myriad of other sources. Galatians 1:10 says *"For am I now trying to persuade people, or God? Or am I striving to please people? If I were still trying to please people, I would not be a servant of Christ."*

Physically, David was no match with Goliath, but he had God on his side. David boldly told Goliath *"You come against me with sword and spear and javelin, but I come against you in the name of the Lord Almighty, the God of the armies of Israel."*

Scripture Reading

1 Samuel 17
Ephesians 6:10-18

Takeaway Questions

David received his strength from the Lord. Thoroughly consider your source of strength. Do you get your strength from yourself, or do you place all your trust in God?

Have you encountered giants in your life? Jot down some of those giants and note how you faced them. Describe your feelings after overcoming a giant or difficulty. Did you experience emotions of relief and joy?

Have there been times in your life that you allowed giants to defeat you and perhaps undermine your faith in God? Explain how you feel about that.

Notes

4

Jonah's Encounter with a Whale

Jonah's Whale of an Encounter

JONAH

Rebellion against God never ends well. When people resist doing what they know God is calling them to do, it affects them and others. Obedience brings blessings and disobedience brings discipline. When God leads us, He is up to something, and we do not want to miss out on that.

The Encounter

The story of Jonah and his encounter with the whale has always captured the imagination of Bible readers. Jonah's story involves multiple

A Clash of Wills
Jonah's story represents a clash between the will of God and the will of man. When there is a clash between man's and God's will; God always wins.

encounters involving rebellion, fleeing from God, bias, and being mad at God.

Jonah was a prophet in the northern kingdom of Israel around the 8th century BC. He had an encounter with God during which God instructed him to go to Nineveh to warn its residents of impending divine wrath. Jonah rebelled against his assignment because of his bias against the Ninevites, who were part of the dreaded Assyrian empire. In his rebellion, Jonah fled from God and boarded a ship bound for Tarshish. In other words, Jonah ran in the opposite direction from his God-given assignment. During his journey at sea, the ship was caught in a fierce storm and Jonah, knowing he was the cause of the storm due to his disobedience, instructed the ship's crew to cast him overboard. At that point Jonah had another encounter, this time with a great fish who swallowed him. After three days in the belly of the fish, God finally was able to get Jonah's attention. Jonah realized he had better obey God and go to Nineveh as instructed. The fish vomited him out onto the shore and Jonah travelled to Nineveh.

After arriving in Nineveh, Jonah successfully preached the message God had given him. The entire city of Nineveh, with 120,000 people, came to repentance after listening to his preaching.

That should have been the end of the story. Jonah, however, lived in anguish, continued in his bitterness toward the Ninevites, and was angry with God. His anger was based on his bias against the Ninevites. In dealing with his anger, he prayed to the Lord. He was angry with God but still called on Him in prayer.

> 2 *"Please, Lord, isn't this what I said while I was still in my own country? That's why I fled toward Tarshish in the first place. I knew that you are a gracious and compassionate God, slow to anger, abounding in faithful love, and one who relents from sending disaster. 3 And now, Lord, take my life from me, for it is better for me to die than to live."*

Jonah 4:2-3

God was merciful and spared the Ninevites, which left Jonah unhappy with God's decision. After his prayerful encounter with God, Jonah went outside the city to wait to observe what he hoped would be its destruction. In other words, he still did not get it. The temperature was hot, and God shielded Jonah from the sun with a fast-growing vine, but later sent a worm to cause it to wither. When Jonah complained of the bitter heat, God rebuked him and scolded him for being more concerned about a vine than about the spiritual condition of the people of Nineveh. Jonah's story shows God's concern and mercy, even for the wicked.

Why was Jonah so reluctant to obey God's instruction to take his message of warning to the people of Nineveh? To better understand that, it is important to know that Nineveh was a major city of the Assyrian Empire. The Assyrians were a cruel, warlike people who were Israel's longtime enemies and had inflicted unspeakable terror on them. To put the relationship between the Assyrians and the Israelites in context, it is important to note that in 721 B.C., Assyria swept out of the north, captured the Northern Kingdom of Israel, and took them into captivity. While it is true that Jonah was a prophet of God, he was also a man with human emotions and feelings. His contempt for the Ninevites was so great that he preferred to see them destroyed than to warn them and give them a chance to repent and be saved.

A Life Application

It is interesting that scholars have spent a great deal of time debating over whether it was a great fish or a whale that swallowed Jonah. There has also been debate on whether the story happened or was a parable. Jesus certainly did not consider the book of Jonah to be a parable.

> *"40 For as Jonah was in the belly of the huge fish three days and three nights, so the Son of Man will be in the heart of the earth three days and three nights. 41 The men of Nineveh will stand up at the judgment with this generation and condemn it, because they repented at Jonah's preaching; and look—something greater than Jonah is here."*
> Matthew 12:40-41.

Jonah is not the only human who has been swallowed by a big fish and survived. There have been at least two documented reports where men have been swallowed by large sea creatures and have lived through the experience. One example is Marshall Jenkins, who was swallowed alive by a sperm whale in 1771 and survived. While arguing over these points, the vital aspect of the story is missed. God can provide a supernatural means of rescue when people are in trouble, and He is compassionate toward all people, even those who are unable to distinguish right from wrong.

Jesus knew Jonah's encounter with the fish was an important example of God's love, compassion, and the need for the obedience of believers in reaching people who need salvation.

Jonah's story of running from an assignment from God and the outcome should teach us important lessons.

Jonah's frustration with God was not based on racism. He was unhappy that God would save a people who had treated his fellow Israelites so brutally.

+ Running from God may be the result of not liking what God wants us to do. Jonah ran from God because he hated the Ninevites. God's assignment included giving his enemies an opportunity for salvation, and that was something Jonah did not want.

+ There is no way to hide from God. Jonah could not hide from God no matter where he went, even in the belly of a whale.

+ God pursued Jonah even when he fled from Him. We cannot outrun our assignments from God.

When He wants us to do something, He will pursue us.

+ Jonah's rebellion led to discipline. He experienced a severe storm at sea and was swallowed by a whale.

God's discipline is not to punish us but to help us to learn from our mistakes. Those who are in Christ receive discipline from our Heavenly Father out of His love for us. The writer of Hebrews focuses on God's discipline chapter 12:5-11.

> *5 And you have forgotten the exhortation that addresses you as sons: My son, do not take the Lord's discipline lightly or lose heart when you are reproved by him, 6 for the Lord disciplines the one he loves and punishes every son he receives. 7 Endure suffering as discipline: God is dealing with you as sons. For what son is there that a father does not discipline? 8 But if you are without discipline—which all receive—then you are illegitimate children and not sons. 9 Furthermore, we had human fathers discipline us, and we respected them. Shouldn't we submit even more to the Father of spirits and live? 10 For they disciplined us for a short time based on what seemed good to them, but he does it for our benefit, so that we can share his holiness. 11 No discipline*

seems enjoyable at the time, but painful. Later on, however, it yields the peaceful fruit of righteousness to those who have been trained by it.

Hebrews 12:5-11

Jonah's story teaches us much about the character of God and how He wants us to view the world. Some Christians have little tolerance for people who do look like or act in the manner they think they should. They seem to forget that God loves all people. People continue to do evil today, not unlike the people of Nineveh in Jonah's day. God loved the Ninevites and wanted them to repent and be saved. He wants the same thing for people today. We are called to love and share the gospel with all people and pray for their salvation. In other words, God desires to give grace, not mete out justice, and uses believers in that process. Sometimes I watch a drama movie that features a bully

Bitterness and resentment are human traits that defeat happiness and contentment. They interfere with relationships with others and, more importantly, with God.

mistreating an innocent person and I become emotionally disturbed. It is my nature to desire retribution to fall upon the bully and vindication to visit the innocent one. I want justice and I want it now. Not grace or mercy, but justice.

As the plot progresses, quite often there is a shift, and the bully has a change of heart. In other words, justice is defeated by grace. That is exactly how God works. He has the capacity to mete out justice, but because of His love and mercy He offers grace. That is why Jesus left heaven to come to earth. It is also why Jesus has not yet returned to earth to redeem it from evil.

> **8 Dear friends, don't overlook this one fact: With the Lord one day is like a thousand years, and a thousand years like one day. 9 The Lord does not delay his promise, as some understand delay, but is patient with you, not wanting any to perish but all to come to repentance.**
>
> 2 Peter 3:8-9

Jonah's experience should cause Christians to examine their thoughts about people. Like Jonah, we are called by God to take His message to others who may live ungodly lives. God is working all around us and is preparing our way. It is up to us to decide if we are willing to share the message of God's love and grace with everyone we encounter or to allow them to be destroyed by their sin. A decision to obey the Great Commission will result in joy and blessings. A decision to disobey will result in discipline as Jonah received when swallowed by the whale. The decision is ours to make.

God extends His love and salvation to every person regardless of social-economic status, race, gender, or nationality.

The book of Jonah is quite revealing. It describes the prophet Jonah's call by God, his flight from that call, rebellion, and discipline. It also shows God's love and compassion for all people. When Jonah rebelled against his assignment, he undermined his relationship with God. When he became obedient, God was able to save a people from destruction. When we obey the assignment given to us by Jesus to take the gospel to the world, we can be an instrument in saving others from eternal destruction. Our options are to either obey or flee.

Scripture Reading

Jonah 1:1-4:11
Matthew 12:38-41
Matthew 28:19-20

Takeaway Questions

Did reading about Jonah's story have an impact on your thoughts about people all around you?

Do you have resentment or anger toward someone? Consider how you can reach out to that person to resolve the issues.

Do you recall a time in your life that you ran from God? Explain.

Jonah was disciplined for disobeying God. What is your understanding of why God disciplines believers?

Notes

_____

_____

_____

_____

_____

_____

_____

_____

_____

_____

_____

_____

_____

_____

_____

_____

_____

5

Ruth's Life-Altering Encounter

Ruth's Encounter with Boaz

RUTH 2

*E*very married person has experienced a first-time encounter with that someone who became their mate. From that encounter, offspring are usually produced and a lineage is extended. God sometimes initiates those encounters. Many people lovingly think of them as being orchestrated by God. There are also encounters between people that are divine appointments aimed at fulfilling God's ultimate purpose. That is what happened to two people who were unlikely candidates for a marital relationship or to be in the Messianic lineage. Those two people are Ruth and Boaz.

Divine Appointments often occur when people are at the end of their own capabilities.

The Encounter

Naomi was a Jewish woman who migrated to Moab with her husband Elimelech and two sons when a famine overtook their homeland of Judah. When she left Judah, she had no way of knowing God was preparing her for a divine purpose. Moab was in what is now Jordan. While living in Moab, Naomi's husband and two sons died. Naomi was left with her sons' wives, Orpah and Ruth. When Naomi learned the famine in Judah had ended, she decided to return home. She asked her daughters-in-law to remain in their homeland, but Ruth refused to leave her, so they travelled to Bethlehem together, arriving during the season of the grain harvest.

> *2 Ruth the Moabitess asked Naomi, "Will you let me go into the fields and gather fallen grain behind someone with whom I find favor?" Naomi answered her, "Go ahead, my daughter." 3 So Ruth left and entered the field to gather grain behind the harvesters. She happened to be in the portion of the field belonging to Boaz, who was from Elimelech's family.*
>
> Ruth 2:2-3

The story gets wonderfully exciting at that point. God, in His infinite mercy for foreigners, widows, and the poor, had instituted laws that governed the harvesting of crops to ensure that no one went hungry.

**9 *When you reap the harvest of your land,
you are not to reap to the very edge of your
field or gather the gleanings of your harvest.* ¹⁰ *Do not strip your vineyard bare or
gather its fallen grapes. Leave them for
the poor and the resident alien; I am the
Lord your God.***

Leviticus 19:9-10

Ruth, as a Gentile Moabitess, went out to glean grain
and entered a field belonging to a man named Boaz. That
was no accident. Of the many fields available to Ruth to
choose from, God led her the field owned by a family
kinsman. The Bible does not tell us how, but Naomi. was
related to Boaz through her husband Elimelech, which
played into the outcome of the story.

When Ruth entered the field of Boaz, she experienced an unexpected, divinely orchestrated encounter that
had implications for the lineage of the Messiah. Only by
reading the entire book of Ruth can one fully appreciate
the full richness of all that God accomplished through
this encounter. One notable part of the story is that Boaz
was the son of Salmon and Rahab. She was once a prosti-
tute, ended up in the linage of the Messiah, and is listed in
Hebrews chapter 11 in what has been called God's Rollcall
of Faith. God's mercies are profound.

Boaz had no idea that God had set him up for a divine
encounter that would change his life and that of Ruth.
They met in his field and eventually were married. Their

marriage produced a son named Obed, who is in the direct lineage of the Messiah.

The encounter between Boaz and Ruth did not just happen. It was a divine appointment, the importance of which became evident eleven hundred years later Mary gave birth to the Messiah. Ruth did not wake up one morning and randomly wander off to find some grain. She was certainly unaware that God was directing her to an important encounter. When Boaz and Ruth encountered one another, it led to a lifetime of love, marriage, and parenthood.

It would be a shame to read of Ruth's story without mentioning how this encounter impacted Ruth's mother-in-law Naomi. Remember, Naomi left her homeland with her husband and two sons to travel to an unfamiliar land. While in Moab, she suffered the tremendous loss of her family. As she arrived back in Bethlehem, scripture paints a strong picture for her emotions. In chapter 1, verses 20-21, Naomi is seen as battling depression and self-pity. She even changed her name to

Naomi moved from the pit of depression to being included in the linage of the Messiah.

"Mara," which means bitterness (opposed to "Naomi," meaning sweet), because she had lost all her male family members. Her life had not been pleasant, and she placed her focus on her disappointments. Naomi's bitterness left no room for joy in her life. Some local women comforted her when they told Naomi that God had not left her without a family. God had provided a redeemer who would renew her life and sustain her in her old age. They told her that her daughter-in-law loved her and was better to her than seven sons. When Ruth met and married Boaz, Naomi moved from a life of bitterness to one of joy and content-ment. It is easy to understand why she felt God had made her life bitter, but it is also wonderful to know that God does not leave us in despair. He is there when we reach the lowest point in our lives. It is interesting that He uses encounters between people to move us from the deepest depression to heights of joy.

A Life Application

I experienced a similar encounter the night I met my husband. I had endured a thirty-year abusive marriage and certainly was not seeking a relationship, but God had other plans. Two mutual friends invited us to meet at their home one evening. They were used by God to set up the encounter that has allowed us to have twenty-four years of life and ministry together. Many of you have had similar encounters, during which God brought you and your life partner together when you were least expecting it. God is always setting up divinely crafted encounters for His people. The key is to be sensitive to how God is speaking to us and leading our paths. As we enter an encounter, we should be aware it may be far more than a random meeting. Often God uses encounters to complete assignments that He has already set into motion. The encounter could be with a person who is suffering and in need of someone who is willing to share a message of hope with them. Remember, it was the women around Naomi who loved and encouraged her. They were sensitive to her emotional state and provided encouragement.

Several years ago, I was with a group of women and when I left, I forgot my coat. I contacted my friend and arranged for her to leave my coat at her church. As I entered the church to retrieve my coat, I had an encounter with the Holy Spirit that spoke to me about attending that church. My encounter with the Holy Spirit resulted in many years of wonderful worship and support I greatly needed as I endured a difficult divorce. Like Naomi, I received support and encouragement from others during a difficult time in my life. It was also there that I encountered a godly man who became my husband and soulmate. Another bonus: my teenaged daughter met a young girl at that church, and they have experienced decades of a best friends relationship. I am absolutely convinced my encounter with the Holy Spirit was a divine appointment that forever changed the direction of my life. I am eternally thankful for that encounter.

God has a way of teaching us lessons through experiences and encounters as we live out our lives. To understand the fullness of that, we should take time to review our past encounters and see how they were God events. When my marriage ended, it seemed like everything was falling apart. At that point, God brought several Christian people into my life to support and encourage me. That has happened many times over the course of my life. I am sure you can say the same thing. God sets up encounters for us to be blessed and to bless others.

Sadly, some people do not fully appreciate how God works in their lives. The closer we walk with God, the easier it is for us to allow the Holy Spirit to guide our footsteps to encounters that matter for His Kingdom. To experience and participate in the ways God is working around us requires us to have an intimate relationship with Him. It is truly a matter of intimacy. Take time to consider how your life is better because of some of the encounters God placed before you. Thank God for those encounters.

Scripture Reading

Ruth 1:1-4:22

Takeaway Questions

Did the reading of the story of the encounter of Boaz and Ruth inspire you to be more intentional as to how you may be of use to God in your encounters?

Have you ever felt the hand of God in helping you with encounters with others?

Did the sharing of my personal encounter with the Holy Spirit remind you of your own encounters with Him and how you and others have been affected? Make some notes.

Naomi's life was positively impacted when other women took time to encourage her when she experienced a state of depression. Christians can be good at helping and praying for people who are physically ill, but often show less concern for others who have emotional and spiritual illnesses. How can you encourage others who are suffering from similar situations?

Notes

6

David's Lustful Encounter

David's Encounter
with Bathsheba

2 Samuel 11

*N*o one is exempt from being tempted by Satan into sinful transgressions. There are many biblical stories of such encounters that should teach us that important lesson. While David truly was a man after God's own heart and was greatly used of the Lord in leading Israel and in writing Scripture, he was not exempted from temptation, failure, and the consequences of sin.

The Encounter

Earlier in Chapter 3, we looked at a high moment in David's life when he encountered the giant Goliath and with God's provision was victorious. Later, we will see David as a man of character when he was pursued by King

Saul. In this chapter, we look at King David's adulterous encounter with Bathsheba and its lamentable outcome. A review of David's encounter with Bathsheba is a lesson on how sin is progressive, one sin leads to others. David kept falling deeper into sin, to the point it led to murder.

Bathsheba was the beautiful wife of a Hittite warrior named Uriah, who served in King David's army. The story of David and Bathsheba reflects an encounter that impacted not only the two of them, but also their family and the nation of Israel. It was an encounter involving the sins of lust, covetousness, deceit, and murder, along with their resulting consequences. David's experience is also a story of God's love, patience, and redemption. It serves as a reminder that God's plans cannot be undermined even by those who sin against Him.

"7 Do not covet your neighbor's house. Do not covet your neighbor's wife, his male or female servant, his ox or donkey, or anything that belongs to your neighbor".
Exodus 20:7

King David's army was away in battle, yet rather than being there leading them he was in the comfort of his palace. He looked down from his rooftop and saw Bathsheba bathing. He then sent for her and quickly that initial lustful encounter resulted in adultery and a pregnancy. To cover the sin of his encounter with Bathsheba, David resorted to lying, plotting with his military commander Joab, and ultimately murder. It is sad how sin spreads like cancer and infects the lives of both the offenders and innocent people.

It did not have to be that way. David started his life as a humble shepherd boy tending his father's flock, then was selected by God to replace Saul as Israel's second king. During that chapter in David's life, he exhibited godly character, even while being pursued by Saul, who was attempting to kill him. He was a man with a heart for God and God gave David supernatural power to overcome Goliath and Saul. David's encounter with Bathsheba exhibited another side of David that had dire lifelong consequences. While he did confess his sin and was forgiven by God, he still had to live with his failure. His actions had ramifications not only for him but also for his family and the nation of Israel. David's family became the very definition for dysfunction that involved rape, incest, murder, and rebellion. His heart desire was to build a temple for the Lord and a shelter for the Ark of the Covenant. God, however, had other plans.

God revealed to David, through the Prophet Nathan, that he must suffer the consequences of his sin with Bathsheba.

David truly did possess numerous attributes. He was a talented musician and poet who penned many of the Psalms, and a leader. David was Israel's greatest king and in the lineage of the Messiah. Even with all those strengths,

In Psalm 51 David lamented over his sin of adultery with Bathsheba. He prayed that God would have mercy on him, according to God's unfailing love and compassion.

he was also a man with human flaws. He allowed his spiritual passion to be overcome by his lustful passion.

David paid for his sin almost every day of his life. He penned Psalm 51 after he was confronted by Nathan. The Psalm is one of pain and regret as David pours his heart out to God. His plea is for forgiveness and for God to be gracious to him. In verse 4, he admits that he has sinned against God. Read the entire Psalm and allow yourself to absorb all the regret and remorse David experienced as one who had failed his Lord. In Psalms 32 and 86, David also pours himself out before the Lord. He recognizes he is a sinner and asks for God's forgiveness and eternal love. He also acknowledges the Lord is a compassionate and gracious God who is slow to anger and abounds in love and faithfulness. He knows God could have struck him down at any time, but he did not. God forgave him immediately upon his confession.

A Life Application

We all experience encounters that place challenges and temptations in our paths. How we respond to those encounters can have profound ramifications, not only for us but also for others. It is important to frequently renew our commitment to being a person with character that pleases God. It is a way to erect defenses against attacks from Satan. David was tempted by Satan and succumbed to that temptation with disastrous consequences.

Over the past several years, several prominent ministries, led by men with a genuine passion for God, have been damaged because of faith leaders who allowed sinful lusts to take control of them. No one should be deceived into believing they are above falling to the luring enticement of the flesh. Satan is a master in using sexual temptation to undermine and destroy the testimony of believers.

There were times during David's life he had a close and intimate relationship with his God. Many of the Psalms he penned demonstrate the intensity and beauty of that relationship. When David penned Psalm 63, he was experiencing a time of personal intimacy with God. One must believe that when David allowed himself to be controlled by his lust for Bathsheba, he had allowed his relationship with God to become stale. Using modern terminology, he was backslidden. To overcome his sin, David had to restore his relationship with God.

This story is a wonderful example of how we also should experience God. David tells God that He is his God, and he eagerly seeks Him. He thirsts for God and he promises to praise Him. David's sin with Bathsheba could not have happened if he had maintained that same intimate relationship with God at that point in his life. Satan is aware of where we are in our relationship with God and exploits it when we drift away from intimacy with our Savior.

Allowing sinful temptation to take control of us during encounters leaves scars that cannot be erased. David was forgiven for his sin, but the remainder of his life was impacted because of his actions. That was not how he wanted to live his life. When you encounter people, do they see Jesus on display or something that is counterproductive for the cause for Christ? After your encounters, are you pleased, or do you lament that somehow you failed your Savior? Encounters leave impressions. How we encounter others speaks volumes about our character, faith and commitment to Christ. Satan uses our encounters with others to try to destroy us and to undermine our witness as Christians. When people encounter Christians, they can be either drawn toward God or repelled from Him. How the encounter is conducted by the believer is often the determinant. Each new encounter is a new opportunity for people to see Jesus.

Scripture Reading

Samuel 11
Psalm 51
Psalm 32
Psalm 86

Takeaway Questions

How did the reading about David's encounter with Bathsheba impact your thoughts about encounters you have? Do you guard yourself from allowing sinful thoughts or actions to interfere with your relationship with Jesus? Take a moment to jot down your thoughts.

Why do you think that David, who has been described as a man who was committed to God's ways and who had fidelity to God's law, allow himself to commit sin with Bathsheba?

Is your relationship with God still fresh or have you allowed it to become stale? What can you do to renew that relationship?

What actions can you take to guard yourself from the inevitable temptations that Satan will entice you with?

Notes

7

A Woman's Touching Encounter

A Woman was Healed by Touching the Hem of Jesus' Robe

MATTHEW, MARK, LUKE

*T*here are people all around us in need of healing. Healing from physical and as well as spiritual illnesses. We were all suffering from spiritual illness until we reached out for a healing that could only come from Jesus. Our healing was the result of faith.

The Encounter

There are several examples of faith found in the Bible in which people touched the hem of Jesus' garments and were instantly healed. One specific example can be found in the gospels of Matthew, Mark, and Luke. Each of these gospel writers tell the story of a woman who had long suffered from a "discharge of blood" who, through faith, "touched the fringe" of Jesus' garment and was instantly healed.

> **6 Wherever he went, into villages, towns, or the country, they laid the sick in the marketplaces and begged him that they might touch just the end of his robe. And everyone who touched it was healed.**
>
> Mark 6:56

The unnamed woman had suffered from a flow of blood for a period of twelve years. She came up from behind Jesus and touched the hem of His garment, believing that if only she could touch His garment, she would be healed. Hers was an encounter with Jesus that was planned and based on the desperation of her condition and faith large enough to believe Jesus could heal her when no one else could. The phrase "an issue of blood" suggests a menstrual issue, but that is not stated. Such a condition would have been a serious problem for a woman living in a Jewish culture where menstruating women were considered unclean. Being perpetually unclean for twelve years could not have been pleasant, as her condition was both physically and religiously problematic.

There is no spiritual infirmity that the touch of Jesus is not able to cure. Jesus can cure even the worst of sinners of all their sins and the spiritual infirmities that were caused by their sins.

Scripture tells us she had been treated by many physicians and had spent all her resources seeking to be healed, without results. As her condition grew worse, she was aware there was no earthly cure for her condition. She needed a cure that only Jesus could provide. The woman had heard of Jesus healing others, and she had faith that He could also heal her. She did not openly approach Jesus to ask for His help, probably because she considered herself unclean. Instead, she joined the crowd surrounding Him and reached out to touch His garment. The moment she touched Jesus' clothing, the fountain of her blood was dried up; and she felt in her body that she was healed.

> **30 Immediately Jesus realized that power had gone out from him. He turned around in the crowd and said, "Who touched my clothes?" 31 His disciples said to him, "You see the crowd pressing against you, and yet you say, 'Who touched me?'"**
>
> Mark 5:3-31

One can only imagine the joy she must have felt when she realized her encounter with Jesus had ended years of suffering. Her approach to Jesus was clandestine, but He immediately knew power had gone out from Him. He turned to the crowd and asked who had touched His clothes. The woman was struck with fear when Jesus turned and looked at her. Matthew tells us she was fearful and trembling, realizing what was done in her, and she came and fell before Him, and told Him the truth. Jesus then called her daughter and told her that her faith had healed her.

Her faith was what healed her. Scripture says Jesus was walking in a crowd of people when this event took place. Many others must have undoubtedly touched Jesus as He walked along, but only the touch of the hem of His garment by this one woman caused Him to realize His power had been affected.

A Life Application

This is a story of both faith and healing. Jesus told the woman her faith had healed her. That comment is worthy of exploration. What, really, is faith? Faith is a word freely tossed around in Christian discussions but is it fully understood, appreciated, and practiced?

+ Faith is the substance of things hoped for, the evidence of things not seen.

+ It is the very foundation of belief. To survive the storms of life everything needs a solid foundation. As Christians, we must have a proper foundation.

+ Faith is belief in God and belief that His word is true. Faith believes God created everything out of nothing. God created man so He could have a relationship with him.

- Faith believes the invisible is more real than the visible.

- Faith is proven by obeying God and His word.

- By faith we come to God.

- By faith we believe God.

- By faith we trust God.

- It is by faith alone that we are saved.

- Faith is a trust that God is bigger than any of our problems. He has our best interest at heart and the power to satisfy that interest.

- True faith is total trust in God. It replaces fear and anxiety and the need for us to try to do things ourselves rather than turn them over to God.

This might be a good time to take a few moments to meditate on the depth of what faith truly is and evaluate how your faith measures up. It is easy to say we have faith when things are going well, but do we have that same level of faith and trust in God during times that are not so good?

The second component of this encounter is healing. Christian songwriter Jeff Switzer has penned a powerful song about Jesus as a healer and His everlasting presence, entitled, *The Healer is Here*. In the song Jesus is the one who heals the sick, raises the dead, and makes the blind see. Whatever you ask for, He is here to help. All we have to do is just reach out and touch Him as He passes by.

Jesus is the healer and is here. People are suffering and need healing that only Jesus can provide. Many are suffering from spiritual afflictions caused by the effects of sin in their lives. Unfortunately, most of them do not realize Jesus is the answer to their problems. The truth is all mankind is spiritually diseased and the only help is Jesus. Just as with this woman, a cure is only available to those who place their faith in Him. There is a need for an encounter with someone who will share the truth of the healing power of Jesus. Like this woman, it remains our responsibility to reach out to Jesus, in faith, to be healed. As the song aptly says, *The Healer is Here*, but for Him to heal there must be an encounter with Him initiated by the one who needs healing. "Just reach out and touch Him as He passes by." That is exactly what the woman in this story did and she was miraculously healed.

As we read the Bible, we should always be asking ourselves the simple question: *How does what I am reading impact my life?* This woman's story should encourage us to plan more encounters with Jesus each day. It should also motivate us to have planned encounters with others who need someone to share His good news with them. He is the only one who can heal their brokenness. How will they know unless they have an encounter with a believer who is willing to tell them about faith and healing?

Scripture Reading

Matthew 9
Mark 5
Luke 8

Takeaway Questions

What lessons did you learn as you read the story of the woman's planned encounter with Jesus?

How strong is your faith? Is it strong enough to believe God can heal your physical and spiritual infirmities? Our lives can be joyful and without anxiety when we place our total faith in Jesus.

What do you think about how Jesus responded to the woman when she told Him she touched His robe?

Notes

8

An Encounter with Denial

Peter's Courtyard Denials

MATTHEW, MARK, LUKE, JOHN

Have you ever been involved in an encounter during which you came away disappointed that you had not been very bold expressing your faith? Perhaps you even evaded the subject of your belief in Christ altogether. Sadly, Christians, have been known to outright deny their faith in Christ. Sometimes believers submit to peer pressure or simply remain silent when being assailed for their beliefs.

Jesus is not surprised by our embarrassment, nor is He unprepared for it.

The Encounter

The Apostle Peter is an interesting character study. At times he was steady as a rock, and at other times he was impetuous and undependable. All four gospels describe a time in Peter's life when he experienced an encounter and was less then dependable. When challenged by unbelievers, he failed to be bold in his faith. In fact, Peter outright denied his relationship with Jesus. He had walked beside Jesus throughout His earthly ministry, listened to His words, watched Him perform miracles, even confessed that he knew Jesus was the Messiah while they were at Caesarea Philippi, and yet when under pressure, he denied Jesus three times in a matter of minutes when questioned concerning his relationship with Him. To make matters worse, Jesus had, only a few hours earlier, told the disciples they would deny Him. He even gave specific details of Peter's denial. *35But Peter declared, "Even if I have to die with you, I will never disown you." And all the other disciples said the same.* It is interesting to note that the story of Peter's denials was penned by all four gospel writers.

As Jesus was being led to a trial before the Chief Priest Caiaphas, Peter followed Him into the high priest's courtyard. It was cold, and Peter joined others around a fire to keep warm. It was there that Peter denied his Lord, just as Jesus had foretold. Then a rooster began to crow, and Peter reached the lowest point in his life. How ashamed he must have been. Peter's denial was based on human frailty. He failed Jesus and the experience of his denial was so devastating to him that he wept bitterly.

Then Peter remembered the word Jesus had spoken: "Before the rooster crows, you will disown me three times." And he went outside and wept bitterly.

Matthew 26:75

In Mark 16, scripture tells us that on Resurrection Morning, Mary Magdalene, Mary the mother of James, and Salome went to the tomb of Jesus with spices to anoint His body and were confronted by an angel who told them Jesus had been resurrected. The angel told the women to go tell the disciples, **and Peter** of the risen Christ. The angel included Peter specifically in the message to the disciples because Jesus had already forgiven and restored him. In John 21 and Luke 5, the gospels

32 "Whoever acknowledges me before others, I will also acknowledge before my Father in heaven. 33 But whoever disowns me before others, I will disown before my Father in heaven".
Matthew 10:32-33

report that Peter received forgiveness and redemption during an encounter with the risen Jesus after a long, frustrating night of fishing on the Sea of Galilee. Peter encountered Jesus, who forgave him and restored him as His disciple.

After his restoration, Peter was a changed man with a new zeal and passion to spread the story of Jesus throughout the Jewish world. His new story really starts in the second chapter of the book of Acts, when he preached a powerful sermon that led three thousand people to become believers in Christ. The Bible does not tell us how Peter died, but church tradition is that he was crucified in Rome. It has been said that when Peter was put to death, he requested to be crucified on an inverted cross because he did not consider himself worthy to die as Jesus had. The weight of his denial remained with him up to his death. That had to be a tremendous burden on his soul.

A Life Application

What can we learn from Peter's denial encounter that will aide in our faith walk? One way we can take heart by reading of Peter's denial is his redemption. There is hope in the knowledge that Jesus is always ready to forgive and restore us when we acknowledge our failure and ask for a renewed relationship with Him. Like Peter, after failing to stand true to our faith, we can use that failure as an opportunity to grow stronger in our faith and witness.

Peter's story is a lesson on human weakness. Even though he had been with Jesus from the very beginning of His earthly ministry, he still failed Him. When Jesus had told Peter that he would deny Him three times that very night before the rooster crowed, Peter, in typical fashion, had boldly proclaimed that would not happen.

To be fair, Peter was not alone in denial that night. Scripture tells us all the disciples were present when Jesus foretold their impending denial, yet they all fled when the time of testing arrived. Jesus understands human frailty. He left Heaven to experience all the challenges that mankind faces on earth. While perfect Himself, He was able to understand firsthand the trials and temptations of life. God had a plan for Peter in His ministry, and He also has a plan for us. The question is: Can we learn from our failures and grow through them to come out the other side as better witnesses for Christ? Peter did, and so can we.

We live in an age that is being described as a post-Christian world where belief in the Bible and living a faithful life brings about ridicule like no other time in history. It is a time of dramatic cultural and spiritual upheaval. Scripture teaches us that spiritual warfare will only increase as the world nears the reappearing of Jesus. When Jesus delivered His message in what is called the Olivet Discourse, found in Matthew 24 and 25, Mark 13, and Luke 21, He warned His followers of a time of tribulation and persecution that will be evident before the ultimate triumph of the Kingdom of God. Public figures are increasingly using their forums to disparage Christians who are serious about their faith. Christians are considered mean-spirited and narrow-minded. The world wants Christians to keep their beliefs restricted to the walls of the church.

In the middle of the first century, the same Peter who had denied Jesus wrote to dispersed Christians who were suffering persecution. In 1 Peter 4:3-4, he described people who were practicing all sorts of sin and their reaction to Christians who abstained from that behavior. Verse 4: **"They are surprised that you do not join them in the same flood of wild living — and they slander you."** When we live righteous lives, our words and actions surprise and intimidate those who choose to live without a relationship with Christ. Peter goes on to describe end time persecution of believers, and his words should encourage us as we live in the ungodly culture today.

I recently heard a powerful sermon in which the speaker called the Church to action and no longer be cowered and silenced. Satan is using his minions to intimidate and quiet the voice of believers. The cause of Christ is losing the culture wars because the Church is allowing itself to be intimidated by the enemies of Christ.

Christians must stand firm and not deny Jesus. It is time for Christians to boldly proclaim that prayer belongs in public places, that abortion of unborn children, same-sex marriage, and sexual sin are just as wrong now as in biblical times. Silence is denial. Satan uses public figures to intimidate and silence followers of Christ. They use the power of mass media and political office to spread lies and intimidate Christians. Jesus spoke about not remaining silent when faced with those who would silence His disciples on Palm Sunday's triumphal entry into Jerusalem, with the crowds loudly proclaiming Jesus as the King who came from God. Some of the Pharisees from the crowd told Him to rebuke His disciples. His answer is as vital today as it was then.

> *"I tell you, if they were to keep silent, the stones would cry out."*
> Luke 19:40

To be faithful to our Savior, we have no other option than to boldly proclaim God's truth. To do otherwise is to do as Peter did when he encountered the embarrassment of denying Jesus.

It is easy to proclaim that we will never deny Jesus when we are not under pressure. Peter never believed he would deny Jesus, but he did.

Let us not suffer bitter disappointment and go out weeping because we have denied Jesus. When we find ourselves denying Jesus, we must repent and ask for forgiveness. He will restore to us the joy of our salvation. Let us loudly proclaim we will not stop being bold as we stand up for Jesus. Christians cannot stand around the fire with unbelievers, warming our hands, and letting them silence us.

Scripture Reading

Matthew 26:69-75
Mark 14:66-72
Luke 22:33-66
John 18:15-27

Takeaway Questions

What did you learn about yourself by reading about Peter's failure and restoration? Take a moment to jot down your thoughts.

Have you experienced encounters in your life when you were less than bold about your faith in Jesus? How did that make you feel?

Did you find encouragement by reading this story? If so, commit notes of the encouragement.

Notes

9

A Woman's
Encounter at a Well

The Samaritan Woman
at the Well

John 4

At times, people develop opinions of others based on cultural rather than spiritual perspectives. Culture creates a world view with biases that God never intended. He created all people in His image and loves them equally. The story of a Samaritan woman's compelling encounter with Jesus at Jacob's Well models Jesus' unbiased love for all people and how He wants His followers to view others.

The Encounter

John did not name the woman, yet her encounter with Jesus is the longest encounter between the Messiah and any other individual detailed in his gospel. John wrote that she was a woman and a Samaritan. That information alone speaks of the universal love of Christ. Women were not considered co-equals with men, and the Samaritans were a race of people traditionally despised by Jews. She also was living a sinful lifestyle. Hers was a holy encounter with Christ that resulted in her eternal salvation and a testimony that convinced many others to believe in Jesus.

The story begins as Jesus was walking through Samaria on His way to Galilee. He sat down to rest around midday at a well in the town of Sychar. That well is known as Jacob's Well because it is believed to have been dug by the Patriarch Jacob. At the well Jesus encountered a Samaritan woman who was coming to draw water. He asked her for a drink, and they entered a conversation that became personal as Jesus revealed who He was and what He knew about the woman and her past. Like all encounters, this could have been little more than casual conversation. It

Around noon, Jesus encountered a Samaritan woman coming to draw water from the well. He asked her for a drink, and their talk took off culminating in her salvation along with many more from her town.

ended, however, in being life-altering, not only for her but also for many others. For everyone involved, it was an encounter that mattered.

Scripture says she was curious and at ease enough with Jesus to ask Him some poignant questions. Her questions, and Jesus' responses, are astonishing. He told her He was the Son of God, the Messiah, and that He had come to offer living water, the kind that will become a spring of water welling up to eternal life inside those who drink. Jesus then shifted to the next phase of their conversation. Not only did He have what she needed, but He also revealed things about her that she was surprised He knew about. She had been married five times and was not married to the man she was currently living with.

After leaving Jesus, she felt compelled to share the news of her encounter with her neighbors. Her life had been transformed and she was excited about it. Can you imagine the joy that entered her life when she encountered Jesus? Those she testified to then came to Jesus, and at their request He stayed in their town two days, talking with them. Because of what Jesus shared with them, many more became believers. Her testimony was instrumental in their salvation.

A Life Application

Christians are often fearful of sharing the gospel because they are concerned they do not know enough scripture. This woman had absolutely no knowledge of scripture, but she did have a personal testimony involving her saving encounter with Jesus. Like the woman at the well, we all have a personal story of our own saving encounter with Jesus. This story displays the importance of believers sharing their testimony as they encounter others. The woman had sin in her life and needed someone to share with her how she could overcome her sin with living water.

During their conversation, Jesus established rapport with her. **Webster's Dictionary** defines rapport as a friendly, harmonious relationship: a relationship characterized by agreement, mutual understanding, or empathy that makes communication possible or easy.

As Jesus spoke with the woman, He provided a lesson on how to share our faith. The most effective method of sharing Christ with others is to first build a relationship with them. Explore who they are by showing interest in them. Jesus already knew everything about the woman, but we do not know about others. To learn about them requires asking about themselves and listening to what they say. When we show interest in others, they are more comfortable with listening to what we have to say about Jesus and salvation. When we empathize with people, they learn to trust us and listen to what we say. Jesus used this encounter purposely.

This encounter demonstrated there is no bias in Jesus' love for mankind. It did not matter that she was female, a Samaritan, or a sinner. He communicated with her as equal conversational partners. Christians must never lose sight of the truth that Jesus loves all people regardless of their societal status. He welcomes all to the kingdom of God. Bias and prejudice are human inventions that targets groups or types of people rather than responding to people as individuals who were created by and loved by God. There is no room for prejudice in the hearts of believers in Christ. Christians should be ruled by humility, obedience, and love for God and for others. Being prejudiced means we consider ourselves better than others. We should be quick to recognize bias as sin and ask the Lord to rid us of it. Culturally, the Samaritans were a race of people who were considered half-breeds. Jesus did not see the Samaritan woman that way. He saw her as a person who was a sinner in need of the living waters of salvation. His encounter with her and her fellow Samaritans demonstrated how He wants us to see people. To God, there are no lesser people, just people who need a life-altering relationship with His Son Jesus.

> *34 So Peter opened his mouth and said:*
> *"Truly I understand that God shows no par-*
> *tiality, 35 but in every nation anyone who*
> *fears him and does what is right is accept-*
> *able to him."*
>
> Acts 10:34-35

The woman's story is one of love, truth, redemption, and acceptance. Jesus accepted her, with all her faults. We all are sinners by nature, but a spiritual rebirth gives us living waters. While all people are sinners, they also are loved by God and in need of redemption. Jesus is ready and waiting to accept everyone.

> *23 For all have sinned and fall short of the*
> *glory of God.*
>
> Romans 3:23

We should consider each new encounter as an opportunity ordained by God. There should be no timidity in sharing the gospel and no reticence created by cultural bias. The way Jesus encountered the woman at the well is a perfect example for each Christian. Encounters can have eternal implications and should be undertaken prayerfully and with purpose.

Scripture Reading

John 4:1-42

Takeaway Questions

What spiritual lessons did you learn as you studied about the encounter the Samaritan woman had with Jesus at the well?

Do you see all people as Jesus sees them, or do you allow the culture surrounding you to shape your views of others? If your world view of people is not what God wants it to be, what can you do to change that?

Like the woman at the well, it should be with great joy that we share with others our personal encounter with Jesus. How often do you share the joy of your faith with people you encounter?

Notes

10

Eve's Encounter with a Snake

Eve Encountered Satan in the Form of a Serpent

GENESIS 3

Most people have an aversion to snakes. We naturally recoil when we encounter even a harmless garden snake. Our relationship with them started in the Garden of Eden at the very beginning of man's existence. The third chapter of Genesis describes mankind's first encounter with Satan and sin, and it involved a serpent. That encounter set in

The story of Adam and Eves fateful encounter with Satan explains the Fall of Man and why sin and misery exist in the world today. Every act of violence, every illness, every tragedy that happens can be traced to that encounter in the Garden of Eden.

motion spiritual warfare on earth that will not conclude until the return of Jesus. The serpent in the garden demonstrates the guile and deception of Satan in his goal to destroy man's relationship with God.

The Encounter

God created Adam and Eve and placed them in the Garden of Eden to care for and nurture the land and to have a loving relationship with Him. Eden is a picture of what the new heaven will be like. No pain, sickness or death existed in Eden until Satan enticed Adam and Eve to commit the first (original) sin against their Creator. God told Adam and Eve they could eat any fruit from the trees in the garden except for the tree of the knowledge of good and evil. He warned them that if they ate from that tree they would die. In other words, Adam and Eve experienced perfect joy and harmony with their Creator until they destroyed all that with an encounter with Satan. Satan began his attack on mankind by using lies. That is still his preferred method of attack. The serpent falsely misled Eve into breaking her relationship with God.

> 4 *"No! You will certainly not die," the serpent said to the woman. 5 "In fact, God knows that when you eat it your eyes will be opened and you will be like God, knowing good and evil." 6 The woman saw that the tree was good for food and delightful to look at, and that it was desirable for obtaining*

> **wisdom. So she took some of its fruit and ate it; she also gave some to her husband, who was with her, and he ate it.**
>
> Genesis 3:4-6

Eve was tempted into violating the sole commandment God had imposed upon her and Adam. The serpent told her she would not die, and that God knew when she ate the fruit her eyes would be opened, and she would be like God, knowing good and evil. It is interesting to note that Satan used the very logic on Eve that caused him to fall from grace. He played to her ego as a weakness and told her she could be like God. Eve fell for Satan's deception during this encounter and believed the tree was not only good for food and delightful to look at, but was desirable for obtaining wisdom. She took some of its fruit and ate it and then gave some to her husband, which he also ate. When she gave the fruit to Adam he was placed in a position where he had to make a choice, either to obey God or do as his wife had told him. Adam's choice was a fateful one. His choice was a direct challenge to God that resulted in dire consequences that we continue to endure thousands of years later.

When God questioned the woman about what she had done, she blamed her actions on the deceit of the serpent rather than her own disobedience. Adam followed suit by blaming Eve. Thus, began a blame game that continues to this day. It is common practice for people to try to excuse their failures by placing the blame on others. Small children learn to use that ploy exceedingly early in life.

Some of the consequences of Eve's failure are:

+ God cursed the serpent.
+ God introduced pain to childbearing for women.
+ God placed labor on man to work for his food.
+ Death and illness entered the world.
+ Sin and evil began the process of destroying mankind
+ Most importantly, man's perfect relationship was undermined.

A Life Application

Eve's encounter with the serpent was only the beginning of Satan's deception and evil in the world. All the crime, hate and destruction that abound everywhere began with one act of disobedience to God. There are serpents all around us. They may not appear to be serpents but that does not diminish their destructiveness. The progression of Satan's deception is unrelenting, and while it may appear to be benign at first, it is always deadly. Because of the seemingly innocent nature of his deception, people entertain encounters with Satan unaware. The Apostle Peter compared Satan to a lion. Experts on the behavior of lions say it is unwise to turn your back and run from a charging lion. By nature, lions run down prey that flee them. By standing firm and facing them, lions become bewildered and confused. In most cases the lion will stop and turn away. The Bible also says we all are like sheep without the ability to protect ourselves against the roaring lion of Satan. That is why God provided us with tools for protection. We can resist the wiles of Satan only by using those tools.

> *8 Be sober-minded, be alert. Your adversary the devil is prowling around like a roaring lion, looking for anyone he can devour.*
>
> 1 Peter 5:8

To contend with and overcome Satan, we must understand how he works and the danger he presents. We must resist him and stand firm in our faith. Our response should never be one of panic, fear, and flight, but a firm resistance through our faith in Christ who is within us.

> *For our struggle is not against flesh and blood, but against the rulers, against the authorities, against the powers of this dark world and against the spiritual forces of evil in the heavenly realms.*
>
> Ephesians 6:12

It is vital to grasp God's heart when He created Adam. Man was created to have a relationship with God that is based on love and obedience. The relationship was to be like a Father and His children. When sin entered man in the garden, it interrupted that relationship. As parents we all desire a healthy relationship with our children. That relationship is dependent on a commitment between both the parent and child. It can be broken when a child rebels against the parent. Broken relationships between parents and children are especially painful. God wants a relationship with us like parents and their children. Try to imagine how God felt when Adam and Eve allowed Satan to deceive them into severing their relationship with their Father and Creator. Eve could have stood up to Satan, but instead she gave him preference over God in her life.

Sin destroys our relationship with our Heavenly Father. Satan does not want us to have a loving relationship with God, so he constantly works to undermine that relationship. To overcome Satan's deception, we must evaluate each of our encounters with others to see how they conform with what our Heavenly Father wants for us. I once had a friend who served on the staff of a church in a counseling ministry. In that capacity, he began counseling a female member of the congregation who was struggling with marital problems. As these counseling encounters progressed, he started to share some of the struggles he was experiencing in his own marriage. Satan entered the process and the two began a relationship that should not have occurred. His ministry and witness were destroyed, and two families were negatively impacted. What started out as an innocent counseling encounter turned terribly bad when Satan introduced a serpent into the equation. My friend's relationship with God was also affected in a negative way.

Our encounters can be defined by what we read, what we watch on television and in the movies, the music we listen to, and the people's voices we permit ourselves to listen to. A few years ago, sermons were being preached from pulpits warning believers about the ungodly material in motion pictures being produced in Hollywood. Today even worse material is entering our homes on television, through computers and smart phones. I have a friend who ministers to preteens and teens, and she is dismayed at the horror stories she finds of young people being controlled by the pornography they are viewing on their electronic devices. A serpent has wiggled his way into the lives of youngsters and an entire generation of young people is being destroyed by Satan through means that did not exist a few years ago. It not only involves pornography, but also sex trafficking, all forms of illicit sexual behaviors, and other ungodly ideas that permeate the minds of our children.

Mass media is increasingly undermining biblical truths by deceptively introducing unholy behaviors into our culture and painting them as normal. Deception even comes from false prophets speaking from church pulpits. What we allow to enter our minds can lead us to accept altered truths and impair our relationship with God. Even Christians watch things on television and in movies they would never have imagined just a few years ago. All these things are serpents being used by Satan to undermine our relationship with our Heavenly Father. Satan uses negative world events to permeate our minds and to discourage us. Christians must concentrate on what is above the world. Negative news should not bother Christians because we know Jesus will bring all the negative in the world to an end someday. In the meantime, we should center our thoughts on Jesus through prayer, Bible study, and removing all distractions that take our focus away from Him. We can concentrate on Jesus by fixing our eyes on Him. If we keep our eyes fixed on God's Word, we can stay above all the negative in the world. Setting our minds on what is above allows us to focus on the eternal rather than the temporal.

During our encounters with people and things, it is useful to imagine that we are not alone. Consider that God is sitting next to us. In truth He really is. Ask yourself: Am I disappointing my Heavenly Father or enhancing my relationship with Him during this encounter? Are our encounters with other people and things spiritually honest or are we being led astray by the deceptive practices of Satan?

To resist crafty deceptive encounters with Satan, we must put on the full armor of God and pray that we will be delivered from the evil one, to immerse ourselves in scripture and in the power that comes from the Creator of the universe. Satan even had the audacity to tempt Jesus. Jesus' response was with quoting scripture. If we walk in close relationship

It is Satan's nature to be deceptive. He has been a liar from the very beginning of time. Satan's first appearance in the Bible comes under the guise of a serpent, who scripture describes as more cunning of all the beasts of the field created by God. He certainly is not a benign cartoon character with a pitchfork.

with the Lord every day of our lives, we are better prepared to resist the temptation to sin. These weapons must be used constantly, or we can be deceived much like Eve was in the Garden of Eden.

Scripture Reading

Genesis 3:1-24

Takeaway Questions

What are some of the subtle and deceptive encounters with Satan that you have experienced in your lifetime? How did you deal with them?

How can you be prepared to recognize Satan's deceptions?

Our modern culture is inundated with deceptive serpents that are luring people away from God. Take some time to consider those deceptions. Note what they are. What can you do to defend against them?

Notes

11

Peter's Encounter with Change

Peter's Encounter with Cornelius

ACTS 10

*T*he book of Acts presents a rich historical account of the first century spread of the gospel that changed the course of history. The ministry of Jesus served as an axis on which God's Old Covenant with the Jews was replaced with a New Covenant that opened a way for all mankind to enter a relationship with God. The idea that God's grace had opened the door for Gentiles to have a relationship with God was difficult for early Christian Jews to fully comprehend and accept. They often attempted to infuse long-standing Jewish religious traditions as an addition to grace. Grace rather than obedience to the law was difficult for them to accept.

The Encounter

In Acts chapter 10, the Apostle Peter was fully confronted with his way of thinking when he had divinely inspired encounters with a vision from heaven, then with a Gentile centurion. A Gentile Roman centurion named Cornelius lived in Caesarea. He and all his family were devout and God-fearing. Scripture tells us that one day Cornelius had a vision (first encounter in this story) during which an angel of God told him to send men to Joppa to bring back a man named Simon (Peter) who was staying there. Cornelius then immediately sent for Peter.

Peter opened his mouth and said: "Truly I understand that God shows no partiality, but in every nation anyone who fears him and does what is right is acceptable to him.

About noon the following day as Peter went up on the roof to pray, he fell into a trance (second encounter). He saw heaven opened and something like a large sheet being let down to earth by its four corners. It depicted all kinds of four-footed animals, as well as reptiles and birds. Then a voice told him to get up, kill and eat. When Peter encountered that voice from heaven, he experienced what might be called a clash of cultures. He responded to the voice by saying he had never eaten anything impure or unclean. The voice then told him not to call anything impure that God had made clean. This encounter forced Peter to accept a radical new truth. All that he had been taught about what was unclean under the Mosaic Law was instantly reordered.

As Peter contemplated the meaning of the vision, Cornelius' emissaries arrived. They told him they had come from Cornelius, whom an angel had told to seek out Peter and listen to what he had to say. The next day, Peter traveled to Caesarea to meet Cornelius who was expecting (third encounter) him. He entered the home of Cornelius and found a large gathering of people. He told them it was against Jewish law for a Jew to associate with a Gentile, but God had revealed to him that he should not call anyone impure or unclean. Peter told them of the new truth that had been revealed to him by God. For the first time he understood that God does not show favoritism and that through the name of Jesus, everyone who believes in Him receives forgiveness of sins.

> *"34 Now I truly understand that God doesn't show favoritism, 35 but in every nation the person who fears him and does what is right is acceptable to him. 36 He sent the message to the Israelites, proclaiming the good news of peace through Jesus Christ—he is Lord of all."*
>
> Acts 10: 34-36

While Peter was still speaking, the Holy Spirit came down on all those present and they were amazed when they saw the gift of the Holy Spirit had been poured out even on the Gentiles. Peter then baptized them in the name of Jesus Christ. His encounter (divine appointment) with Cornelius was used by God to transform his worldview from everything he had been previously taught by religious leaders to a new reality. There was no longer an Old Covenant that restricted access to God to only Jews. The law had been replaced by grace available to all people through the ministry, death, and resurrection of Jesus.

A Life Application

People generally address change based on information provided to them. We are all faced with encounters throughout our lives that have the potential to change our way of thinking based on new information. Change can be either good or bad. For Christians, how we deal with change depends on how grounded we are in our faith and our understanding of God's Word. When we accept Christ, everything we once believed is instantly changed.

It seems like there has never before been a time in history when mankind has been bombarded with so much cultural change. A great portion of that change deviates from our Christian beliefs and heritage. These changes can be both challenging and confusing. What people once believed is now being rejected because they are being infused with new information. Information is not always truth. Even human sexuality is being redefined on a massive scale. As believers we must evaluate all these cultural changes against the truth of scripture. Peter had an encounter with an angel that guided his beliefs. We have the Bible to function as our guide to truth. To eliminate confusion requires us to be fully immersed in the Bible. Is what being said consistent with God's Word? We have also been given the Holy

Spirit to help us discern truth from lies. If our worldview is not firmly rooted in the truth of God's Word and the leadership of the Holy Spirit, we are susceptible to being deceived during our encounters.

Peter's encounters in Acts 10 required him to accept a new and a better way. He had lived his entire life religiously following the Ten Commandments and 613 Levitical laws, but now he accepted the truth that grace had replaced all that. The change Peter experienced was orchestrated by God and was for good, while much of the change we are confronted with today is from Satan and is for evil.

There are two basic applications for Christians facing cultural change today. To sift through all the change, we must clearly know what is from God and what is not. One thing is certain: if it is not from God, it is from Satan. That may sound simplistic, but it is the truth. Our first reaction to ungodly change usually is to complain about it. I often hear conversations about how bad things are getting, but seldom do I hear words about taking action to counter it. Complaining never alters reality. What is needed is action. That action requires us to understand the reality of the changes that are happening, pray for deliverance, and become involved in countering false narratives.

We must understand that people are embracing ungodly change because they are unaware of its destructiveness. Satan is deceiving people, which leaves them unaware of what is occurring. Today's cultural change is causing the world to sink deeper into darkness, sin, and depravity. What is needed is light that can only come from Jesus. He gave us an assignment to bring the light of truth to the world. The need has never been greater for people to hear God's truth. Christians must engage people and provide them with biblical truth. That cannot happen when we limit their associations with other Christians. People are being given information on a massive scale that claims to be truth, but it is a lie. The only way for people to know truth is for it to be shared with them.

It is no wonder that people are being deceived when they know nothing about God and His Word. I will never forget an encounter that my husband and I had with a waitress. As the waitress took our order, we told her we were about to pray over our food and asked her if she had anything she would like us to pray for. We were astonished when she said she had no idea what prayer was. After explaining prayer to her, she asked us to pray for her brother who was in the military and about to begin a tour of duty in a war zone. There is no way to know how that encounter affected her, but at least she was introduced to prayer and God's love. People like that are easily swayed by the lies being spread in modern culture. How could they not be?

The Holy Spirit sets up encounters as divine appointments. Our responsibility is to be sensitive to what He is doing in our midst. We can make a difference in today's anti-Christian culture by engaging in Spirit-led encounters with people who desperately need to hear about Jesus.

Scripture Reading

Acts 10:1-48
Acts 15:1-29
Hebrews 8:6-13

Takeaway Questions

Acts 10 offers a glimpse into an entirely new belief system that involved a cultural change of view for Peter. What did you learn from these encounters? Take a moment to jot down your thoughts.

The world is changing at a pace never before seen. Most of that change is ungodly, and people desperately need an encounter with someone who will share Jesus with them. How often do you do that? How can you do more to counteract the cultural shift away from God?

Notes

12

A Widow's Encounter
with a Man of God

The Widow at Zarephath's Encounter with The Prophet Elijah

1 Kings 17

$\mathcal{M}$ost people are drawn to great drama stories that involve trials and tribulations of life. They tend to be the bestselling books, movies, and plays. There are many encounters described in the Bible that also play out as human drama. In 1 Kings chapter 17, there is a true drama of epic proportions. It tells the story of the Prophet Elijah being used by God to save the lives of a widow and her young son.

The Encounter

The Prophet Elijah had an encounter with God, who instructed him to take a trip, drink from a brook, and eat food supplied by ravens. Verse 6 says the ravens brought him bread and meat in the morning and bread and meat in the evening, and he drank from the brook. God supplied Elijah's needs much like He did for the Israelites in their forty-year sojourn in the wilderness after leaving Egypt. His provision was provided by God one day at a time. Elijah took his encounter with God seriously and did all that he was instructed to do.

The brook eventually dried up and Elijah had another encounter with God, during which he was told to travel to the Phoenician city of Zarephath in the region of Sidon, where God had directed a widow to supply him with food. Jesus recounted this encounter in Gospel of Luke.

The provisions of God for His people are seen throughout the Bible. Whether it is for land, food, or shelter God provides for those who follow His commandments.

> **"25 But I say to you, there were certainly many widows in Israel in Elijah's days, when the sky was shut up for three years and six months while a great famine came over all the land. 26 Yet Elijah was not sent to any of them except a widow at Zarephath in Sidon."**
>
> Luke 4:25-26

Elijah had been rejected by the Jews, so God gave him a mission to go to a Gentile city. Similarly, the Jews rejected the Messiah, so God opened the door for Gentiles to have a relationship with Him. When Elijah arrived at Zarephath he encountered a widow and asked her for some water and a piece of bread. Verses 10 and 11 appear to indicate the widow was unaware that she had been prepared by God concerning her encounter with Elijah. That is the way God often works. He has a mission for us and leads us by the Spirit to do something we are unaware of.

The widow told Elijah she did not have any bread. All she had was a handful of flour in a jar along with a little olive oil in a jug and she was gathering a few sticks to take home and make a meal for herself and her son, fully expecting it would be their last meal. The drama then intensified. Elijah told her not to be afraid, but to go home and do as she had said. He told her to use her limited provision to cook a meal for him. After doing that she was to make something for herself and her son.

> *"The flour jar will not become empty and the oil jug will not run dry until the day the LORD sends rain on the surface of the land."*
> 1 Kings 17:14

The widow faithfully did exactly as Elijah had instructed her and there was daily food for Elijah and the woman's family. Later her son became ill and stopped breathing. In her sorrow she became troubled with Elijah. He stretched himself out on the boy and cried out to the Lord, to let the boy's life return to him. God heard Elijah's cry, and the boy was revived. She then knew for sure Elijah was a man of God.

There are three important encounters described in 1 Kings chapter 17. First, Elijah had two separate encounters with God. During those encounters Elijah had two choices: he could fail to do as God instructed or he could be obedient. As a man of God, he chose to trust God and do as he was told. His decision to be obedient during these encounters allowed him to be an instrument of God in the lives of the widow and her son. They undoubtedly would have died without God's intervention through Elijah. What must have been going through her mind? Most people would have told Elijah to go away and leave her alone, but she did as he instructed. Her willingness to comply with his request saved her and her son from starvation.

The widow does not appear to have been originally a worshipper of Jehovah. She lived in a heathen country, and probably was herself a heathen: but she obeyed Jehovah's servant. She did his bidding, and doubtless became a true follower of the living God.

It is revealing how God even works through encounters between believers and unbelievers. What matters is the willingness of believers to use encounters as divine appointments to reach unbelievers with the gospel message. The widow had no way of knowing that she had been prepared for a divine appointment with a stranger that would save her life and that of her son.

A Life Application

When Christians experience encounters with others, they should take a moment to consider them as possibly being divine appointments. Once we accept that notion, we can better understand the importance of entering encounters with spiritual purpose. The widow's encounter with Elijah was a lifesaving encounter and the remainder of her life would never be the same. Christians are sent by God on missions to tell others about Him. When we share the saving power of Jesus, we can help others encounter an eternal lifesaving experience. Just as God prepared the widow for her encounter with Elijah, He still prepares unbelievers for encounters with His people who are prayerfully ready to share the gospel. The Holy Spirit prepares the heart for the habitation of God before anyone comes to Jesus for salvation. It is the job of believers to build upon what has already been done by the Holy Spirit. As He prepares the hearts of others, He also prepares the hearts of believers who are in tune with the Holy Spirit and are willing to act. There is no greater joy than to lead a lost person to a saving relationship with the Lord. Elijah acted on his instructions from God and a heathen widow had her physical life saved and she entered a newfound belief in God. We all can and should be used like Elijah was in this story. The story of the widow's encounter with Elijah has all the makings of a great drama. It involved impending tragedy, dire circumstances, trust, and salvation.

Like Elijah, we have been commissioned by God. It should be noted that every encounter we face involves choices. For them to be effectual, we should pray for God's wisdom to lead us. People's hearts are being prepared by the Holy Spirit and they are often unaware of it.

That was what was happening to the widow. His preparation requires someone to make the next move by sharing the gospel. When it happens as God wishes, there is always a happy ending. Otherwise, the ending can be tragic. As believers, we are a critical component. Take to heart that Jesus left us with the Holy Spirit to guide and help us.

> *"For the Holy Spirit will teach you at that very hour what must be said."*
>
> Luke 12:12

Scripture Reading

1 Kings Chapter 17
Luke 4

Takeaway Questions

Did reading of these encounters teach you anything about how you can be His instrument in fulfilling His work in your community?

Have you experienced a blessing by helping someone in need? Note that.

How did you see God working through Elijah to meet the needs of the widow and her son?

Notes

13

*Joseph's Encounter
with Temptation*

Joseph Encounters Potiphar's Wife

GENESIS 39

*T*emptation to sin is a constant in everyone's life. The best way to avoid falling into a trap of allowing yourself to be enticed by sin is to decide what kind of character you want to have as a man or woman, and to have a constant, intimate relationship with the Lord Jesus. Joseph is one of the favorite biblical characters of all time and his life has been an inspiration for believers throughout the centuries. There is no telling how many preachers have preached messages entitled "From the Pit to the Palace," describing how Joseph went from being thrown into a pit and sold into slavery by his brothers, to becoming one of the most powerful men in Egypt. Joseph's story is one of twists and turns, some might call detours, that demonstrate that life does not always follow a straight path and is not always easy.

Lives seldom track a path imagined in youth. God had a plan for Joseph's life and there were probably times when he questioned what God was doing. That thought must have been in his mind when his brothers sold him into slavery. This study is just a snippet of Joseph's life, but it is vitally important because it reveals what powerful temptation Satan can place in people's lives, even those who are believers in Christ. Temptation like Joseph experienced can reveal the nature of character and the depth of one's relationship with God.

The Encounter

Genesis chapter 39 describes events while Joseph was living in Egypt. One of Pharoah's officers named Potiphar had bought Joseph from Ishmaelites who had brought him there. Joseph's brothers had sold him into slavery out of jealousy. Even though he was a slave, God was with Joseph, and he became a successful man. He served in the household of his master who could see the presence of the Lord in

When resisting encounters involving sexual sin, the best defense is to be armed with the Word of God.

Joseph's life. Potiphar had made Joseph his personal attendant and placed him over his household and everything he owned. The Lord blessed Potiphar because of Joseph.

Scripture says Joseph was well-built and handsome. While in Potiphar's service, he had several encounters involving sexual temptation with Potiphar's wife. How he responded, revealed the strength of his character. She looked longingly at Joseph and said, "Sleep with me." The allure of sexual temptation has been the downfall of people since the beginning of time. It has destroyed families and even the personal witness of Christians who have fallen into its trap. Men with powerful ministries have succumbed to illicit sexual encounters that not only destroyed their ministries and families but also sent many of their followers into discouragement and disbelief. It took courage, but Joseph rejected Potiphar's wife's advances.

> *8 But he refused. "Look," he said to his master's wife, "with me here my master does not concern himself with anything in his house, and he has put all that he owns under my authority. 9 No one in this house is greater than I am. He has withheld nothing from me except you, because you are his wife. So how could I do this immense evil, and how could I sin against God?"*
>
> Genesis 39:8-9

Potiphar's wife was not deterred and continued her attempts to seduce Joseph, but he continually refused to have a sexual encounter with her. His refusal was based on his character and his commitment to both God and to his master, Potiphar.

Unfortunately, standing up for what is right can provoke dire consequences that seem unfair. That is what happened with Joseph. One day Potiphar's wife grabbed him by his garment and again attempted to seduce him. He left his garment in her hand, and he fled. His continued rejection of her turned into a quest for vengeance. She lied to her husband by telling him that Joseph tried to seduce her. Potiphar became furious and had Joseph thrown into prison, where he experienced years of pain. Eventually redemption occurred for Joseph that impacted the lives of millions of people, including his own family. It seems unfair that people like Joseph, who are dedicated to faithfully serving God, suffer pain and even death because of their commitment to Him. The reality is that God has a master plan we often fail to understand. The lesson from Joseph's experience is that his suffering was the path to life and redemption for millions of people. With that said, an important question we must ask ourselves is: How much are we willing to endure by remaining people of faith and integrity?

A Life Application

Encounters can involve many different circumstances and outcomes. The story of Joseph and Potiphar's wife involved Satan using one of his greatest tools to try to destroy God's work through sexual temptation. For both men and women, encounters involving sexual temptation can be destructive for those involved and for innocent bystanders. Entire families are often destroyed by sexually immoral encounters. Joseph exhibited tremendous character in rejecting the enticement in his encounters with Potiphar's wife. It is also important to note this is not a story of a single encounter. She continued her pursuit, which certainly placed additional pressure for him to succumb to her enticement.

Satan uses human weakness to destroy people and is a master manipulator and persistent adversary. Potiphar's wife was direct in her attempts to seduce Joseph. Quite often sexual temptation is less direct. It can start out an innocent, friendly encounter that opens the door to the development of feelings that end in sin. Joseph's response to temptation to sin was to flee from it. David allowed himself to succumb to it with Bathsheba. He permitted his carnal nature to draw him into sin that resulted in a damaged relationship with God.

"No temptation has overtaken you that is not common to man. God is faithful, and he will not let you be tempted beyond your ability, but with the temptation he will also provide the way of escape, that you may be able to endure it."
I Corinthians 10:13

Joseph's response is one all God's people should follow: he fled from it. The best way to avoid temptation is prevention. As much as possible, Christians should avoid situations that Satan can use as a foothold. Many times, people place themselves in situations where temptation can easily arise. Both men and women should carefully control their circumstances. Places where they meet, who is involved, and the nature of permitted conversation are important considerations when avoiding temptation. What may seem innocent encounters can turn destructive if not properly prepared for. A casual lunch with a business associate or fellow employee can be used by Satan to introduce temptation. He knows our weaknesses and is prepared to attack them.

It is also always good to have an "exit strategy" in place as a method to respond to encounters with temptation. Be alert to the potential for temptation and plan how you will respond if it comes. I am reminded of the old hymn, *Just a Little Talk with Jesus.* When faced with temptation, just have a little talk with Jesus.

Joseph was a man of character. When temptation arose, his character was his defense. A good way to

Sometimes there are unintended consequences for doing the right thing. We must always make God honoring decisions regardless of the consequences

avoid falling into the trap of temptation is to decide what kind of character you want to have as a man or woman. As you encounter temptation, ask yourself what a person of strong character should do. A Christian's character must be founded on God's Word and a strong relationship with God that includes a persistent prayer life and a committed habit of Bible study. Temptation is inevitable in life, so be prepared for it.

Scripture Reading

Genesis 37:1-45:28

Takeaway Questions

What are your thoughts about Joseph's character and integrity? How are your thoughts impacted by what appears to be the unfair punishment Joseph was forced to endure because of his integrity?

Are you prepared to do what is right even though that could result in a painful outcome? Note your response.

What are your thoughts about integrity and principles as they relate to how Christians should live their lives?

Notes

14

Philip's Encounter with An Angel

Philip Receives Instructions
from an Angel

ACTS 8

*H*enry Blackaby and Claude King have authored a wonderful study entitled, ***Experiencing God — Knowing and Doing the Will of God.*** The study's main purpose is to point out that God is working all around us and it is our job to be so spiritually perceptive that we can see where God is working and to join in Him in that work.

Acts chapter 8 records the story of an encounter Philip had with an angel of the Lord who presented him with instructions for a trip he had not planned to take. While his was an encounter with an angel, the Holy Spirit does the same thing the angel did.

The Encounter

The angel in Philip's story gave him instructions that did not reveal the purpose for his trip. However, he did not question them. Philip had faith to believe that if he obeyed the instructions given by the angel, God would guide his footsteps. As it turned out, the trip involved a divine appointment with a eunuch who needed help in understanding Isaiah's prophecy concerning the Messiah. The Holy Spirit was convicting the eunuch, but he needed someone to help him understand what it all meant.

God is real, and His angels are real. The Lord really does send them to intervene for people in times of need. Some encounters with angels are very overt, while others are more subtle.

The angel only told Philip which way to travel; all else would be taken care of by God. Along the way, he encountered a eunuch who was an important Ethiopian official. The eunuch had gone to Jerusalem to worship and was on his way home. When Philip encountered him, he was sitting in his chariot reading the book of Isaiah the Prophet. The Spirit told Philip to go to that chariot and stay near it. He ran up to the chariot and heard the man reading Isaiah the prophet. Philip asked him if he understood what he was reading. The eunuch's response was ***"How can I,"* he said, *"unless someone explains it to me?"*** He invited Philip to sit with him. He was reading Isaiah's prophecy of the death of Jesus, and he asked Philip to tell him who the prophet was talking about. Then Philip told him the good news about Jesus. As they traveled along the road, they came to some water and the eunuch asked to be baptized. They went down into the water and Philip baptized him. When they came up out of the water, the Spirit of the Lord suddenly took Philip away, and the eunuch did not see him again, but he went on his way rejoicing.

A Life Application

This is a story of how God orchestrated a divine encounter. Philip must have been euphoric as he led this man to Jesus. He had no idea what his day would bring until he had an encounter with the angel of the Lord who presented him with his divine appointment.

Billy Ray lived his life in gratitude that Jesus had saved him when he had reached his lowest point. After his encounter with Jesus, Billy Ray was seated on the mountaintop, joyfully experiencing God's daily assignments for him.

A few years ago, I was blessed to meet a man named Billy Ray whose life was dedicated to serving the Lord. Billy Ray was a Texas cowboy who had lived a hard life and had spent years in prison. While in prison, Billy Ray had an encounter with Jesus that was nearly as radical as Saul's was on the Damascus Road. He also encountered another hardcore prisoner who had also experienced his own encounter with

Jesus while in prison. That man has since become a powerful man of God who leads a ministry for troubled souls.

When I met Billy Ray, he had been a Christian for a few years and was deeply involved in ministering to people, and in particular, men and women who were incarcerated. Each morning, Billy Ray would find a quiet place to read his Bible and to earnestly pray for an assignment from God. His was not simply a brief quiet devotional time but rather an extended period of worshipping his Savior and seeking divine instructions. Billy Ray lived in a day tight compartment. In other words, he lived one day at a time and was only concerned with what God had instore for him each day. Not long after I met Billy Ray, he suddenly was called to heaven. I had the honor to attend a memorial service for my friend, and what a blessing that was. For hours people lined up to testify as to how Billy Ray's testimony and living example had impacted their lives and pointed them to Jesus. Numerous prisoners, wearing prison clothes, strode to the podium, holding their Bibles high over their heads and beginning their testimony by boldly proclaiming what Billy Ray had taught them **"This is my Bible, my Bible is my road map."** I have never attended a memorial service that left my soul so filled. It was truly a celebration of the life of a man, saved by grace, who dedicated his life to reaching others for Jesus and experiencing the joy of his salvation.

Philip did not wake up that morning expecting an assignment from God that day. Billy Ray, on the other hand, pleaded with God each morning for his daily divine assignment. Billy Ray told me God never failed in providing an assignment and that each assignment blessed him as much as he could possibly have blessed others. His life was enriched by the encounters God orchestrated for him. His joy in Jesus was immeasurable. God was working on the Ethiopian eunuch, and because Philip was obedient to the instructions given him by the angel, he was blessed to lead a man to a saving faith in Jesus. Little did Philip know he would meet the eunuch that day, nor did the eunuch know God was sending someone to help him understand what he was reading.

Philip's story should be an important lesson for modern Christians. As Blackaby and King have written, God is still working all around us. People live with all kinds of anxiety and are searching for answers. They desperately need an encounter with Jesus. The church, like everything else, has recently been impacted by a worldwide health pandemic. The nature of how the church functions has changed, and as a result the church has moved more away from the shell of the sanctuary and out into the world where people live. God has awakened the Church to a new urgency. There are wonderful new opportunities to become involved in His work. Those opportunities involve personal encounters during which we can share the gospel. The question is: Are we ready to seek encounters that may involve divine encounters? Perhaps someone you encounter today, like the Ethiopian eunuch, is quietly seeking an answer to spiritual questions and is being prepared for a life-changing encounter with anyone who is willing to share the good news of Jesus. The world is full of people who need help with finding answers to spiritual questions. Christians can be that help by starting each new day praying for a divinely prepared encounter.

Philip's encounter is an example of what can happen when time is invested in the lives of others. There are people all around us who are in desperate need for someone to invest in them. With the right commitment and sensitivity to the workings of the Holy Spirit, we can share the joy of leading others to Jesus. He will order our steps just as He did for Philip.

Scripture Reading

Acts 8:26-40

Takeaway Questions

Did Philip's encounters with the Angel of the Lord and the Ethiopian eunuch impact your thinking about encounters in your life? Take a moment to jot down your thoughts.

Did you develop a new perspective for your own quiet time by reading of Billy Ray's morning search for God's assignment, one day at a time? If so, note your thoughts.

Do you take time to consider each encounter you have as a possible divine appointment? How can you be more intentional in your encounters with others?

Notes

15

Jesus' Wilderness Encounter

Jesus' Encounter with Satan in the Wilderness

MATTHEW 4

In the early chapters of the gospel written by Matthew, he describes the beginning of the earthly ministry of Jesus. He moved from His baptism in the Jordan River to His testing encounter with Satan in the wilderness. Jesus was led by the Spirit into the wilderness to be tempted by the devil. The baptism of Jesus was an early high point in His ministry. As He arose from the Jordan River, He heard His Heavenly Father say, *"This is my beloved Son, with whom I am well pleased."* From that spiritual high, Jesus was immediately tested by Satan after He had fasted forty days and nights and was hungry.

The Encounter

> 3 *Then the tempter approached Him and said, "If you are the Son of God, tell these stones to become bread."4 He answered, "It is written: Man must not live on bread alone but on every word that comes from the mouth of God."5 Then the devil took Him to the holy city, had him stand on the pinnacle of the temple, 6 and said to Him, "If you are the Son of God, throw yourself down. For it is written: He will give his angels orders concerning you, and they will support you with their hands so that you will not strike your foot against a stone." 7 Jesus told him, "It is also written: Do not test the Lord your God." 8 Again, the devil took Him to a very high mountain and showed Him all the kingdoms of the world and their splendor. 9 And he said to Him, "I will give you all these things if you will fall down and worship me."10 Then Jesus told him, "Go away, Satan! For it is written: Worship the Lord Your God and serve only Him." 11 Then the devil left Him, and angels came and began to serve Him.*

Matthew 4:3-11.

The wilderness encounter between Jesus and Satan is a classic clash between good and evil. Jesus had just experienced a spiritual high as He was baptized and heard the voice of His Father in Heaven commending Him. He moved from that high point to a period of fasting and solitude in a wilderness. After forty days of fasting, He was obviously hungry. Enter Satan, the master of all temptation. His first attempt to tempt Jesus was to offer bread to relieve His hunger, then used ego and materialism.

How Jesus resisted Satan during their wilderness encounter reveals a pattern for believers to follow. All people experience the temptation to sin and to disobey God. Jesus showed the best way to respond. He resisted with the help of God and his Word. The Lord's encounter with Satan in the wilderness occurred for our sake.

There is the obvious question: How could Satan possibly believe he could defeat the very Son of God? The answer probably lies in his belief that he can prevail over God. While Jesus was fully God, He also was fully man, able to sympathize with the reality of temptation. Satan probably believed he could convince Jesus, the man, to succumb to the desires of the flesh.

To defeat Satan, Jesus quoted scripture and Satan left Him.

A Life Application

This story provides a powerful lesson for everyone about how to address encounters with Satan. First and foremost, no one is immune to Satan's temptations to sin. Even the Son of God experienced an encounter with Satan that involved temptation, but He chose to be obedient to the Father. Jesus used the most effective weapon to combat Satan. He chose to quote God's Holy Word. Jesus' encounter in the wilderness reinforces the fact that Satan is always trying to destroy people. Peter warned us to be alert because the devil is our adversary and is prowling around like a roaring lion, looking for anyone he can devour.

Satan appeared to Jesus and tried to tempt Him to sin. Jesus having refused each temptation, the Devil then went away, and Jesus returned to Galilee to begin his ministry.

We must never lose sight of the fact that spiritual warfare is ever present. It is a battle between good and evil that will not end until Satan is cast into hell forever. Christians must resist Satan and remain firm in their faith.

Jesus faced His adversary during His wilderness encounter at the very beginning of His earthly ministry. What better time for Satan to destroy believers than when they are new in the faith and not fully grounded in God's Word? That should encourage believers to mentor new believers and help them grow in their strength to overcome Satan's crafty encounters. He knows our points of weakness and uses those times to test us. Sometimes even our spiritual mountaintop experiences leave us vulnerable to Satan's testing. He knew Jesus was hungry, so his first attempt to deceive Him was to offer food. When that failed, he tried a temptation involving pride. Satan challenged Jesus to throw Himself from a high place, knowing God would send His angels to catch Him. The third temptation concerned lust of the eyes. Satan showed Jesus all the kingdoms of the world and its splendor, while offering it all to Him if He would worship him.

The Apostle Peter warned us, we must be prepared for encounters with Satan and be ever ready to resist him, just as Jesus was. Satan is always rebuffed by God's Word. Jesus responded to each

In each temptation, Jesus responded with God's word. This is how we should respond to temptations as well.

temptation beginning with three words: "It is written." Jesus found power in quoting the Hebrew Scriptures, which He had been studying since He was a boy. He knew scripture by heart and was fully prepared to quote from it as He did often throughout His earthly ministry. That is a lesson we should learn from this example provided by Jesus. To be effective as Christians, we must know God's Word and always be prepared to quote it as a rebuff to Satan. We have been instructed to keep God's Word ever present on our lips and meditate on it day and night, so we will be able to do what is written in it. Psalm 119:11 *says,* **"I have treasured Your word in my heart so that I may not sin** *against You.*" Hebrews 4:12 says the Word of God is living and effective and sharper than any double-edged sword, that you can take your stand against the devil's schemes. In Ephesians 6, Paul wrote to put on the full armor of God. Part of that armor is the sword of the Spirit, which is the Word of God. The more scripture we have placed in our hearts and minds, the better prepared we are for ungodly encounters.

It takes more than just reading scripture. To become fully immersed in it we must meditate on it and pray over it. We are weak vessels who need to get our strength from God. Without a firm grounding in God's Word, we are vulnerable to evil encounters. Many of those encounters are disguised and may appear to be innocent. A thorough understanding of God's Word is a sure way to unmask those seemingly innocent encounters. It allows us to see what truth is and expose the lies that abound in our world. There can be no misconception, the same Satan who encountered Jesus with enticing promises is still ever present in our world. The only way to stand up to him is with the help of Almighty God. All power comes from the Lord.

Scripture Readings

Matthew 4:1-11
1 Peter 5:8-9
Ephesians 6:10-18
Joshua 1:8

Takeaway Questions

Jesus defeated Satan's attacks with a powerful stab of God's sword—the Word of Truth. When you are tempted, do you battle it with the truth of the Bible, or do you try to defeat it with your own inadequate willpower?

Have you ever quoted scripture during an encounter? Jot down the circumstances as you remember them.

What did the encounter that Jesus had with Satan teach you about how Satan works?

Notes

16

David's Encounter with an Adversary

David's Cave Encounter with King Saul

I SAMUEL 24

ife can involve encounters with adversaries. They can be a true test of character. King Saul's jealousy of David caused him to try to kill him many times. David had every right to fight back and to protect his life, yet he refused to do so. Saul had been anointed by God to be the first King of Israel. David had no desire to harm Saul or be

"Do not repay anyone evil for evil. Give careful thought to do what is honorable in everyone's eyes. If possible, as far as it depends on you, live at peace with everyone. Friends, do not avenge yourselves; instead, leave room for God's wrath, because it is written, Vengeance belongs to me; I will repay, says the Lord".
Romans 12:17-19

his adversary, as he honored and respected his position and authority.

The Encounter

1 Samuel 24 describes an incident in a cave during which David had an opportunity to kill Saul, but spared his life. Saul had been told that David was in the Desert of En Gedi, so he took three thousand men and went to look for him. Along the way, Saul entered a cave to relieve himself. David and his men were far back in the cave. His men reminded him that the Lord had promised to give Saul into his hands to deal with as he wished. Then David crept up unnoticed and cut off a corner of Saul's robe. He became conscience-stricken for having cut off a corner of his robe.

> **6 He said to his men, "As the Lord is my witness, I would never do such a thing to my lord, the Lord's anointed. I will never lift my handagainst him, since he is the Lord's anointed."**
>
> 1 Samuel 24:6

This encounter demonstrates a time in David's life when he displayed character that was not evident in his encounter with Bathsheba. He exited the cave, called out to Saul and bowed and prostrated himself with his face to the ground. He told Saul what had happened in the cave and that he would not lay a hand on the king, because Saul was the Lord's anointed. He further told Saul he had not wronged him, even when Saul was trying to take his life. When Saul realized what had happened, he wept aloud. and said to David:

> *"17 You are more righteous than I, for you have done what is good to me though I have done what is evil to you. 18 You yourself have told me today what good you did for me: when the Lord handed me over to you, you didn't kill me. 19 When a man finds his enemy, does he let him go unharmed? May the Lord repay you with good for what you've done for me today."*
>
> 1 Samuel 24:17-19

A Life Application

David showed strength of character in the manner in which he dealt with his adversary. Saul had been seeking to destroy him and, in the cave, David had the opportunity to avenge all the wrongs that had been done to him by Saul. He also had pressure from his men to kill Saul. We all have people around us who freely offer their unsolicited advice. It is important to filter all advice we receive to ensure it conforms with God's expectations. David could easily have done what his followers advised him, yet it was not in his spiritual nature to do what most people would have done. David allowed himself to be controlled by his spiritual nature rather than his carnal nature. The very nature of man results in people doing wrong to others. We all experience it. Some people allow the wrongs in life to undermine their joy. They even can go so far as to exact revenge. Others live defeated lives as they allow hurtful feelings to dominate them and their outlook on life. A good question to ask ourselves is: Does the wrong done to me rise to the level of the wrongs done by Saul toward David? Even more so, do the wrongs approach the level of wrong done to Jesus as He was crucified? Remember, He prayed to the Father that they be forgiven. Has the person tried to kill you? Saul had tried to kill David, yet he treated Saul with kindness and respect. Allowing ourselves to wallow in self-pity over a perceived wrong only harms ourselves.

Another lesson learned from David's encounter with Saul is to respect authority. Remember that Saul had been anointed by God to be king over Israel. David knew he must respect that anointment. Church members some-times have deep disagreements with their pastors. When they choose to criticize the pastor, they are disrespecting the anointment of God. The Bible provides a method of addressing disagreements that must be followed. If, after following the biblical procedure, the dispute remains, it must be turned over to God. Only God can appropriately address the issue. Far too many fellowships have been destroyed because parishioners showed disrespect toward God's anointed.

It is interesting that Christians often call on others to respect authority, then show disrespect to people who should be respected. Even more disturbing is that they usu-ally do not even see the dichotomy between their words and their actions.

As a result of the cave encounter, Saul realized his actions toward David had been wrong and wept aloud. He acknowledged that David was more righteous than he was, and he had treated David badly. It is man's nature to handle problems by ourselves. God, on the other hand, wants us to turn everything over to Him and trust in His ability to properly address our issues. We all are human and as such have a carnal nature. For that reason, it is always best for us to turn situations over to God. If left to our own devices, the outcome would not be pretty. Too often we allow our egos to reign over us rather than give situations to Jesus and trust Him for the proper answer. When we treat people with kindness and respect, even when we have been wronged, we allow God to take care of the situation. If we harbor ill feelings, anger, and bitterness toward others, we allow Satan to take control over our lives. We end up being the real losers. The teachings of Jesus place much emphasis on forgiveness.

> *43 "You have heard that it was said, Love your neighbor and hate your enemy. 44 But I tell you, love your enemies and pray for those who persecute you, 45 so that you may be children of your Father in heaven. For he causes his sun to rise on the evil and the good and sends rain on the righteous and the unrighteous. 46 For if you love those who love you, what reward will you have? Don't even the tax collectors do the same? 47 And if you greet only your*

> **brothers and sisters, what are you doing out**
> **of the ordinary? Don't even the Gentiles do**
> **the same? 48 Be perfect, therefore, as your**
> **heavenly Father is perfect."**
>
> Matthew 5:43-48

In Matthew 18, Peter asked Jesus how many times he must forgive a brother or sister who has sinned against him. Note, Peter is asking about the failure of a fellow believer, not an unbeliever. He asked if he needed to forgive the person seven times. Jesus responded in verse 22, *"I tell you, not as many as seven, but seventy times seven."* Jesus' response to Peter was that we are not to limit our forgiveness to any fixed number of times.

To be sure, other people will fail us, and while that may hurt, it is an inevitable element of human nature. Not to forgive has a negative impact on the unforgiving person. Lest we forget, harboring unforgiveness is a sin that interferes with experiencing an intimate relationship with our Savior. We are reminded as we take the Lord's Supper to search our hearts.

> **Let a person examine himself; in this way**
> **let him eat the bread and drink from the cup.**
>
> 1 Corinthians 11:28

As we examine our hearts, unforgiveness is a detriment to approaching the sacrament in a pure, undefiled manner. When you consider the lesson that can be learned from David's encounter with his adversary, consider the following:

+ Start with forgiveness.
+ Pray for those who have abused you, rather than living with bitterness or seeking revenge.
+ Steven prayed to God for forgiveness for those who were stoning him to death.
+ Remember, Jesus forgave those who were about to crucify Him.

Forgiveness is not easy, but with God all things are possible. Life is happier and richer when we release all feelings of bitterness and revenge. Revenge always results in heartache and pain. Forgiveness brings joy and peace. David did not live with a spirit of bitterness and desire for revenge, and neither did Joseph. He could have applied revenge to his brothers for selling him into slavery, but he did not. Instead, we are shown his heart in Genesis 45:15, *"Joseph kissed each of his brothers as he wept, and afterward his brothers talked with him."*

Because we are human, the lessons from David's encounters with Saul are not always easy to live out. Our culture exploits the notion that everything is about "me." The example set by David, and more importantly, by Jesus, is to love and respect even those who do not treat us as we feel we should be treated. It is always about Jesus and never about us.

Scripture Readings

1 Samuel chapters 18-28
Ephesians 4:26-27
Matthew 6:14-15
Colossians 3:13

Takeaway Questions

Have you ever struggled with your feelings toward someone who had mistreated you? How did you address those feelings?

Consider that everyone you encounter has a different personality and set of beliefs that can result in hurt feelings. Saul's rage and jealousy are contrasted by David's forgiveness and respect. How do you feel about that?

David showed respect for Saul because he was the king and had been anointed by God. Do you always show respect for those in positions of authority, and especially for those who have been called by God for His service? How can you do better?

Notes

17

A Leper's Thankful Encounter

Ten Lepers Healed, One Gave Thanks

LUKE 17

*T*here are many stories in the New Testament that describe Jesus miraculously healing people of all kinds of maladies. He even raised several people from the dead. In Luke 17, we find the story of ten lepers being healed during an encounter with Jesus. This encounter involved faith, obedience, a healing experience, and a lesson about showing gratitude.

The Encounter

Jesus was traveling along the border of Samaria and Galilee when ten lepers called out to Him, asking that He have pity on them. They needed healing from their dreaded disease. Jesus responded by telling them to show themselves to the priests. The lepers showed obedience and did as Jesus had instructed. They probably were expecting Him to immediately heal them on the spot as He had with so many others. When that did not happen, they still showed faith and believed in Him. The lepers then went to the priests and were cleansed from their disease.

If the story had ended there it would be a great example of faith and healing, but that is not what happened. One of the ten lepers, a Samaritan returned and was so thankful that he threw himself at the feet of Jesus to show his gratitude. The healed leper was bold in how he thanked Him. Jesus told him his faith had made him well, and because he returned

The Israelites believed that leprosy was both punishment for sin and divine curse because it was a chronic and incurable disease that was highly contagious. Lepers were societal outcasts who lived in colonies separated from society.

to thank and praise God, he would also receive a spiritual healing. This added blessing of salvation is especially tied to the man's faith. His faith had not only sent him to Christ for healing, but it also sent him back to praise and thank Him.

It is sad that only one of the ten lepers who had been healed returned to express gratitude. It is also interesting to see that the one who returned was a Samaritan, a race despised by the Jews. As with His encounter with the woman at the well, Jesus showed care and compassion for a Samaritan.

17 Then Jesus said, "Were not ten cleansed? Where are the nine? 18 Didn't any return to give glory to God except this foreigner?" 19 And he told him, "Get up and go on your way. Your faith has saved you."

Luke 17:17-19

One must wonder about the nine who did not return to Jesus to express their gratitude. God gave all ten a chance to do what was right. Perhaps they failed because their hearts were not right. Maybe they just were apathetic. The Samaritan gave thanks because his heart was full of gratitude. All of them were healed, but the nine missed the blessing the Lord gave to the man who returned to give thanks. They all believed that Jesus could heal them, but nine did not take time to let Jesus know how much they appreciated what He had done for them.

A Life Application

This encounter displays the importance of being grateful and thankful for what God does for us. Gratitude and thankfulness are important elements of every human's wellbeing, yet it is an unfortunate truth that most people struggle with expressing gratitude. We live in a culture that has an attitude of entitlement instead of thankfulness. Being thankful is more than a feeling, it requires us to live lives with thankfulness and gratitude. People crave to hear the words "thank you," and are often disappointed when they do not hear those two important words. We are not entitled to the blessings we receive from God. They are gifts we should be thankful for. His greatest gift is His love and compassion toward us.

Parents are disappointed when children do not take time to express their gratitude. There is a joy that abounds in their hearts when they hear the words "thank you" and "I love you," coming from those they love. I have granddaughters who often send cards that express thankfulness for all my husband and I do for them and their families. It is always heartwarming and fills my heart with joy to receive those cards.

It is disappointing, however, when people fail to show gratitude. Several friends have shared with me their disappointment that their children and grandchildren seldom take time to thank them. God also craves to hear His children show gratitude.

For some people, showing gratitude is a natural attribute. For others, it is something that is foreign to them. For them to express gratitude is something they must work at. When we develop a habit of showing gratitude, it becomes a way of life that benefits us and those around us. A spirit of gratitude, and the outward expression of that spirit, brings joy to everyone involved. Developing a spirit of thankfulness also makes us heathier people; mentally, spiritually, and physically. The two simple words, "thank you," have a profound impact on our daily perspective and our ability to be happy. Researchers have found that people who are more grateful have better heart health and more disease-fighting cells in their bodies. Giving thanks has a benefit of keeping bitterness out of our lives. Thankfulness and bitterness cannot co-exist in the same person.

During His time on earth, Jesus was a man with human feelings. Imagine how He must have felt when nine people He had healed from a dreaded disease failed to show gratitude. How do you feel when you do something for another person, and they do not care enough to say thank you? Even a small expression of gratitude goes a long way in lifting the spirits of those who do things for us.

People live defeated and discouraged lives because they permit bitterness to control them. Bitterness is apparent in their very countenance. A cure for bitterness is forgiveness and gratitude. A victorious and happy life requires both.

Christians have so much to thank the Lord for. He healed us from our sins by taking them on Himself when He willingly allowed Himself to be crucified. How often do we take time to fall on our knees and tell Him how thankful we are for what He has done for us? Like the lepers, He has healed us from a dreadful disease, sin. The Bible is replete with messages concerning thankfulness and gratitude.

> **And let the peace of Christ, to which you were also called in one body, rule your hearts. And be thankful. Let the word of Christ dwell richly among you, in all wisdom teaching and admonishing one**

another through psalms, hymns, and spiritual songs, singing to God with gratitude in your hearts. And whatever you do, in word or in deed, do everything in the name of the Lord Jesus, giving thanks to God the Father through him.

Colossians 3:15-17

Give thanks to the Lord, for he is good; his faithful love endures forever.

Psalm 106:1

Give thanks to the Lord, call on his name; proclaim his deeds among the peoples.

Psalm 105:1

And let the peace of Christ, to which you were also called in one body, rule your hearts. And be thankful.

Colossians 3:15

Our God is a loving Father who blesses us beyond measure. He is deserving of our thankfulness and gratitude. By being thankful to Him, we mature in ways that allow us to bless others and enrich our own lives. Take time to think about your own life. Are you thankful for what God and other people have done in your life? Do you show and tell God and others how much you are thankful for them? Of greatest importance is letting Jesus know every day that we are grateful for what He has done for us. His sacrifice for you extends into eternity. Your relationship with Jesus will be far more beautiful as you learn to thank Him with all your heart.

The one leper who thanked Jesus was a blessing to the Lord. He wondered about the nine but was uplifted by the one.

Scripture Readings

Luke 17:11
1 Thessalonians 5:16
1 Chronicles 16:34
Psalm 9:1
Colossians 3:16

Takeaway Questions

Are you more like the one or more like the nine lepers? Do you tell the Lord how thankful you are for all the blessings He bestows on you?

How you show more gratitude to God.

Are you a person who finds it difficult to show thankfulness and gratitude to others? If so, what can you do to improve that?

Notes

_____

_____

_____

_____

_____

_____

_____

_____

_____

_____

_____

_____

_____

_____

_____

_____

_____

_____

_____

_____

18

An Encounter with Looking Back

Lot's Wife Looked Back

GENESIS 19

$\mathcal{C}$hristians have been saved from a life of sin and separation from God. A life in Christ is full of hope for the future and joy. A past without Christ has no value to it. There is every reason to look ahead to the future and no reason to peer back into the past.

The Encounter

In Genesis 13 Abraham and his nephew Lot, along with their families, separated. The separation was a mutual decision because the land was insufficient to support two large herds of sheep and because they had herdsmen who feuded with one another. Abraham settled in Canaan and Lot settled in Sodom. After their separation, Abraham was visited by three men, God and two angels, who told Abraham and Sarah they would have a son in their old age.

God also told Abraham that He was about to destroy the cities of Sodom and Gomorrah because the people's sin there was so great. Abraham asked God if He would sweep away even the righteous along with the wicked.

Abraham pleaded with God to save Sodom from His wrath because there were some righteous people living in the city. His petitions started with a plea to spare the city if fifty righteous people could be found there. He then pleaded his case down to ten righteous people.

In chapter 19 two men (angels) arrived in Sodom in the evening as Lot was sitting at the gateway to the city. He got up to meet them and invited them to his home. He prepared a meal for them and before they went to bed, the men from Sodom surrounded Lot's house. They demanded that he send his house guests outside so they could have sex with them. He went outside to confront the men and begged them not to do such a wicked thing. He even went so far as to offer them his two virgin daughters. The visiting men of the city told Lot and his family to get out of Sodom because it was going to be destroyed. The two men led Lot, his wife and two daughters safely out of the city and one of the men told them to flee for their lives and **do not look back.** They were to flee to the mountains, or they would be swept away.

Lot and his family fled to Zoar, arriving there before the sun had risen. The Lord rained down burning sulfur out of the heavens on Sodom and Gomorrah, destroying all those living in the cities. But Lot's wife did what she was warned not to do, She looked back, and became a pillar of salt. She was turned into a pillar of salt as she looked back because she disobeyed the precise instruction given by the angels not to look back to Sodom. Her action suggests that she identified more with the sinful people of Sodom than she did with the God who had saved her and her family.

Her failure to flee God's punishment becomes a vivid warning to others. She experienced a cata-strophic encounter with looking back. Scripture offers many examples of the importance of looking forward to a life serving Christ and of the cost of looking back to the sinful life you have been saved from.

Paul wrote in his letter to the Colossian church to set their minds on things above, not on earthly things. Put to death what belongs to your earthly nature: sexual immorality, impurity, lust, evil desire, and greed, which is idolatry.

A Life Application

There is a tendency for people to emotionally identify with their known past. While the future is unknown, it has promise and hope for those in Christ. For Christians, the past is filled with sin and failure, but the future is glorious as we are filled with the Holy Spirit. Christians should let go of their past but also use it as a tool to learn from our past poor performances and decisions. As I wrote in Chapter 1, Paul's past allowed him to experience things that were preparing him for his God-given assignment. Most of us have past experiences that can be used in our testimony as we warn others of the consequences of sin. I recently read that a quick glance into the past for the purpose of personal evaluation is important. It is like looking into the rearview mirror of your car. But, when that glance becomes a constant gaze, you are in trouble. Christians should never be tempted to focus on their sinful past. The Bible repeatedly warns believers to focus on their bright future in Christ. The encounter of Lot's wife when she looked back was due to her identification with the culture of the two cities, not to prepare for a work for God. It should be a lesson for all believers of the consequences of looking back to the life of sin. Sodom represented the worst that sin offered, but it was what she was familiar with.

Christians are instructed to set their hearts on things above, not things of the world. Our journey must always be facing forward toward Christ. God's direction for our lives is for us to look forward, knowing His will is perfect and He will be present with believers each step of the way. Farmers keep their eyes focused straight ahead when plowing a field or the rows would not be straight. The Apostle Paul used an analogy of running a race to describe the Christian life in Hebrews 12, and the author added, "keep our eyes on Jesus."

> *1 Therefore, since we also have such a large cloud of witnesses surrounding us, let us lay aside every hindrance and the sin that so easily ensnares us. Let us run with endurance the race that lies before us, 2 keeping our eyes on Jesus, the pioneer and perfecter*

> *of our faith. For the joy that lay before him,*
> *he endured the cross, despising the shame,*
> *and sat down at the right hand of the*
> *throne of God.*
>
> Hebrews 12:1-2

Believers in Jesus must constantly keep our eyes on Him. Do not look back or to the right or left. The Apostle Paul commented on this in his letter to the Philippian church.

> *"13 Brothers and sisters, I do not consider*
> *myself to have taken hold of it. But one*
> *thing I do: Forgetting what is behind and*
> *reaching forward to what is ahead, 14 I*
> *pursue as my goal the prize promised*
> *by God's heavenly call in Christ Jesus".*
> Philippians 3:13-14

There is a wonderful hymn that says, "Turn your eyes upon Jesus, look full in His wonderful face, And the things of earth will grow strangely dim, In the light of His glory and grace."

When Lot's wife had an encounter with looking back, she violated the instructions that had been given by the angels. When she looked back, it led to her destruction. Disobedience to God's instruction always leads to discipline. Jesus reminded His disciples in Luke 17:32 of what happened to Lot's wife and the consequences of looking back. Keep looking forward toward Jesus. Our future ahead is glorious as we pursue a life in Christ. The past offers us nothing but disaster, just as Lot's wife found out.

Scripture Readings

Genesis 19
Luke 9:62
Isiah 43:18
Proverbs 4:25 -27

Takeaway Questions

Are you ever tempted to look back on the life you lived and the people you shared life with before your conversion to Christ? If the answer is yes, how do you react to that experience?

Do you understand why God wants His people to focus on their future and their hope in Him? Explain.

How can you do more to keep your eyes on the future walking with Jesus?

Notes

19

Encounter with The Holy Spirit

Encounters with the Holy Spirit

Acts 2

*One of the most intriguing studies in the Bible is the Holy Spirit and how He works. Before Jesus ascended to heaven, He told His disciples He would send a Counselor, also known as the Holy Spirit, Paraclete or Holy Ghost. While the Holy Spirit was sent as a counselor in Acts 2, it must be understood that the Holy Spirit is part of the Triune God and therefore has always existed. There are numerous Old Testament references to the work of God's Spirit. The first reference to the Holy Spirit is found in the second verse of the Bible.

> ***Now the earth was formless and empty,***
> ***darkness covered the surface of the watery***

> ***depths, and the Spirit of God was hovering***
> ***over the surface of the waters.***
>
> Genesis 1:2

The Holy Spirit was sent to do many things, be a comforter to believers and to convict people of sin and a need for repentance. He also empowers believers to maximize their relationship with the Father and to fulfil His purpose in their lives. When Jesus ascended into heaven, mankind encountered a heavenly companion in the Holy Spirit.

The Encounter

Near the end of the Passover meal, immediately preceding His crucifixion, Jesus told His disciples He was going away, and He would ask the Father to give them another Counselor to be with them forever. (Jn. 14:16). In Acts chapter 1, Jesus ascended into heaven, then in Acts chapter 2 the Holy Spirit appeared just as Jesus had promised. The Holy Spirit is part of the Triune God. Just like the Father (God) and Jesus (Son), the Holy Spirit is eternal (Heb. 9:14), omnipotent (Gen. 1:2), omniscient (1 Cor. 2:10-11), omnipresent (Ps. 1:3, 9:7-10), holy (Rom. 1:4), and life (Rom. 8).

When the Holy Spirit came onto the scene on the Day of Pentecost in Acts 2, His presence was immediately and powerfully felt. Those present witnessed miraculous things never seen before and Peter was emboldened to preach the gospel and three thousand people were saved.

A Life Application

As people give their lives to Christ, the Holy Spirit takes up residence in their hearts. He comes alongside of us and guides our paths throughout life. He is an ever-present companion. For the Holy Spirit to perform His work, He must be perfect and therefore of deity and equal to God the Father and Jesus Christ.

It is important to grasp just how the Holy Spirit works to appreciate all He offers believers as they live out their lives.

The Holy Spirit confirms our relationship with our Heavenly Father.

This is how we know that we live in him and he in us: He has given us of his Spirit.
1 John 4:13

"Nevertheless, I am telling you the truth. It is for your benefit that I go away, because if I don't go away the Counselor will not come to you. If I go, I will send him to you. When he comes, he will convict the world about sin, righteousness, and judgment."
John 16:7-8

The Holy Spirit assists us in our prayers.

He helps us align our prayers with the will of God and God will always do what is in line with His will.

> *In the same way the Spirit also joins to help in our weakness, because we do not know what to pray for as we should, but the Spirit Himself intercedes for us with unspoken groanings. And He who searches the hearts knows the Spirit's mind-set, because He intercedes for the saints according to the will of God.*
>
> Romans 8:26-27

The Holy Spirit reveals the truth of scripture

> *When the Spirit of truth comes, he will guide you into all the truth. For he will not speak on his own, but he will speak whatever he hears. He will also declare to you what is to come.*
>
> John 16:13

God is revealed to us through the reading of scripture. That revelation comes from the Holy Spirit. He opens our minds to understand the Word of God. We cannot understand what we are reading unless the Holy Spirit teaches us and imparts meaning to us. Reading the Bible should always be about understanding what God is revealing to us, not receiving education like reading a history book.

The Holy Spirit helps overcome sin through His power.

We are unable to overcome sin in our own power. We need the Holy Spirit if we are to win a victory over sin. God sent Him to do that for us.

The Holy Spirit provides boldness to witness

> *"But you will receive power when the Holy Spirit has come on you, and you will be my witnesses in Jerusalem, in all Judea and Samaria, and to the ends of the earth."*
>
> Acts 1:8

He not only provides boldness but can even tell us what to say. He wants to give us the boldness to be a witness for Christ. With His help, we walk with confidence and boldness, unashamed or unafraid to identify with our Lord and Savior. All we must do is ask.

The Holy Spirit convicts us of our sins.

The word *convict* is an English translation of the Greek word *elencho*, which means "to convince someone of the truth; to reprove; to accuse, refute, or cross-examine a witness." In essence, the Holy Spirit acts much like a spiritual prosecuting attorney who exposes evil, reproves evildoers, and convinces people they need a Savior. Conviction is far more than a guilty conscience; it is a divine call to repent of sin and accept salvation. It is a ministry of the Holy Spirit that reveals the Gospel and calls for a saving faith. To have a saving relationship with Jesus requires an encounter with conviction and a response to that conviction. He comes alongside of us and guides our paths throughout life. He is an ever-present companion. As our constant companion, the Holy Spirit knows the state of our relationship with God and calls believers to repent from sin and failure when necessary. We must allow the Holy Spirit to rebuke, correct, and train us, as we are *"transformed into the same image from glory to glory"* (2 Cor. 3:18).

The Holy Spirit gives us spiritual gifts

Christians have been given gifts from the Holy Spirit that enable them to better serve Christ and to live more fruitful lives.

> *But the fruit of the spirit is love, joy, peace, patience, kindness, goodness, faithfulness, gentleness, self-control. The law is not against such things. Now those who belong to Christ Jesus have crucified the flesh with its passions and desires. If we live by the Spirit, let us also keep in step with the Spirit.*

> Galatians 5:22-25

Living in lockstep with the Holy Spirit makes us not only better and more powerful Christians, but also better people. Consider all the attributes listed in Galatians

5:22-25 and you cannot help but notice that anyone who possesses those attributes is a powerful example of someone who truly is Christlike.

One of the works of the Holy Spirit is a call to action for believers. **Webster's Dictionary** defines a calling as "a strong inner impulse toward a particular course of action especially when accompanied by conviction of divine influence." An encounter with a call to act can be a prompting to become involved where God is working.

A couple of years ago, my husband sensed that God was calling him to join others from our church in taking a short-term mission trip to Guatemala. He also felt that same calling several years earlier to serve on a mission trip to China. As with any trip to a third world country, he experienced physical discomfort, but that was far outweighed by the joy he received in joining what God is doing in those countries. God uses His own to reach out to people who otherwise would not know about Him.

I have also felt the calling of the Holy Spirit to use my experience as a survivor of domestic abuse to minister to women who live in daily fear of those who should love and protect them. I am brokenhearted by their stories of personal and emotional distress, but my trials with domestic abuse prepared me for a mission to help others.

God uses the Holy Spirit to minister to believers through encounters such as reading their Bible, praying, and meditating. He lays on our hearts a need to respond to what He is saying to us. The Holy Spirit uses conviction to elicit confession of sin, at other times it is a call to fulfil an assignment from God. Most believers have heard others use the term, "I am convicted to do something." That is exactly what it is, a calling or conviction. Christians must be open to hearing the Holy Spirit calling them to act. The Holy Spirit can only be effective in us when we give Him full access.

Every person who has accepted Jesus as their personal Savior has experienced an encounter with the Holy Spirit. That must not be our only encounter with Him. Earlier, I discussed how the Holy Spirit works. For Him to perform those works effectively, we must give Him full and total access to our hearts and lives. It is the key to living an effective life as a believer. When we give Him that access, we grow spiritually, have a more effective Bible study life, a more powerful prayer life, and make ourselves available to being involved where God is working around us. He opens our spiritual eyes to see what He calls us to do. The believer should never underestimate the power and influence of the Holy Spirit. Yet, the believer should always respect the co-equal position of the members of the Godhead and not elevate one member over the other.

Scripture Reading

John 16
Ephesians 4:3
Luke 5:8
Acts 2:4:47

Takeaway Questions

Do you recall a time when you felt the convicting power of the Holy Spirit to confess your sin and accept Jesus as your personal Savior? Take some time to make notes of that encounter and review those notes periodically to refresh your commitment to Jesus.

When Jesus ascended into heaven, He sent the Holy Spirit to come alongside us to guide and comfort us. His intent was for the Holy Spirit to be our constant companion. Do you walk through life in a close companionship with the Holy Spirit? If not, what can you do about that?

Have you experienced the Holy Spirit calling you to take action for kingdom purposes?

Notes

20

Encounters with Uncomfortable Truths

Encounter with Truth

HEBREWS 4:12

*T*his review of encounters is different. It does not focus on a single or personal encounter. It is about encountering truth. Truth is something we all seek to know and understand. To satisfy that need, we must understand it can only be found in God's Word, in prayer and being filled with the Holy Spirit. We live in an age when truth is being manipulated. God is unchangeable and so is His Word. Culture may try to create an altered version of truth, but anything other than God's Word is not truth.

"When the Spirit of truth comes, he will guide you into all the truth."

John 16:13

The Encounter

The world encountered truth with the incarnation of Christ. He was born and came into the world to bear witness to the truth, the unchanging absolute truth of God. Jesus spoke truth to the very end of His time on earth. While questioning Jesus leading up to His crucifixion, Pilate asked if He were a king, and Jesus responded:

> *"You say that I'm a king," Jesus replied. "I was born for this, and I have come into the world for this: to testify to the truth. Everyone who is of the truth listens to my voice."*
>
> Matthew 18:37

Pilate's response to Jesus shows he was in the same quandary as most people are today. *"What is truth?"*

Much has been written about the encounters people had with Jesus that involved healing, feeding the hungry, and observing His miracles. There are also many stories in which people who encountered Him were

Truth is revealed in The Bible in both the Old and the New Testament. God's law and promises are the absolute standard of all truth.

forced to face the uncomfortable truth of His message. We all want to focus on the things that make us feel at ease and comfortable, but that is not always in our best interest.

Jesus always spoke truth and the truth often caused people to shy away from Him. His was a mission to reveal truth, not to entertain crowds.

A Life Application

What is truth? One dictionary definition of truth is "a verified and indisputable fact." Truth has become situational in today's culture. Society is redefining truth in ways that blame Christianity for all the problems that surround us. That is what first century Jewish religious leaders were guilty of. Regardless of what culture chooses to accept, God's Word is the <u>only</u> truth. It is impossible to have conflicting truths. It is either truth or a lie. Truth often makes others feel uncomfortable, but truth cannot be altered simply to make people comfortable. Speaking the truth made Jesus unpopular with many people and it still makes Christians unpopular today. When we confront people with the truth of the Bible, we interfere with their comfort zone. People who stand on biblical truth today are called inflexible, mean-spirited, and intolerant. Truth brings light into a dark world. Those who live in darkness do not want an encounter with truth that exposes their sin. A vital, uncomfortable truth is that no one can have a relationship with God and have eternal life, unless they choose to follow Jesus and reject the lies with which Satan has saturated the world.

> *6 We are from God. Anyone who knows*
> *God listens to us; anyone who is not from*

> *God does not listen to us. This is how we*
> *know the Spirit of truth and the spirit of*
> *deception.*
>
> 1 John 4:6

Bible truths are timeless and are never situational. It is not a smorgasbord where people can choose what truth they want to believe. People focus on Jesus' words about love and compassion and not about sin, discipline, punishment, and hell. They have been seduced by the spirit of the age. Jesus spoke more on eternal judgment than anyone else in the New Testament.

Faithful followers of Jesus must love people enough to have truth-sharing encounters with them. It may not be easy, but must be done. First century religious leaders crucified Jesus for speaking truth that challenged their beliefs. The apostles spread biblical truth throughout the world even though it made them outcasts. The Old Testament prophets consistently told truth as it was given them by God. They did not tickle people's ears with soothing messages. Speaking truth that had been revealed to them by God cost many of the prophets their lives. That did not stop them. Like the modern world, Old Testament Hebrews chose to believe in lies rather than accept truth that required uncomfortable actions.

Hearing the truth that sin is wrong makes people uneasy, but unless they experience an encounter with truth, they will never understand the saving grace that Jesus provides. In Mark 10, a rich man was saddened to hear the truth that to become a follower of Jesus he had to sell his wealth and give to the poor. He went away sad because he had great wealth and was not willing to give it away. He valued his wealth more than a relationship with Jesus. When he encountered an uncomfortable truth from Jesus, he decided to live with comfortable lies.

In Matthew 16:24-26, Jesus told His followers becoming His disciples requires a denial of self. Whoever wants to save his life will lose it, but whoever loses his life because of Jesus will find it. In the first chapter of his letter to the church in Rome, Paul did not mince words in proclaiming the truth of sin. He wrote that because of people's sin, God let them continue their shameful lusts and receive the due penalty. Paul provides an extensive list of their sins in that chapter. People often limit their view of Romans 1 to sexual perversion, but Paul does not stop there. He expands the discussion to include numerous sins that Satan encourages people to commit. Be careful not to miss what Paul says in verse 32. They not only practiced sin but also applauded others for practicing sin. Does that sound familiar? Today's culture idolizes sinful people. Truth so greatly needs to be told.

> **29. *They are filled with all unrighteousness, evil, greed, and wickedness. They are full of envy, murder, disputes, deceit, and malice. They are gossips, 30 slanderers, God-haters, arrogant, proud, boastful, inventors of evil, disobedient to parents, 31 undiscerning, untrustworthy, unloving, and unmerciful. 32 Although they know***

full well God's just sentence — that those who practice such things deserve to die — they not only do them, but even applaud others who practice them.

Romans 1:29-32

People have always committed sins that violate the truth of God's Word. They choose to remain in their sin by accepting Satan's lies and rejecting God's truth. Modern culture is rife with the belief that there are no absolutes and that whatever you choose to believe can be your personal truth.

Even some religious organizations that claim to be Christian have also been duped into accepting and propagating false narratives. Truth cannot be manipulated. There is only one truth, and it is the standard by which God judges the world. Jesus left us with a commission to take His message to the world and that message includes sharing God's truth. In no time in history have so many people lived with the need to hear the truth — no Satanic spin, just biblical truth.

Christ did not come to bring peace. He came to bring war on sin, to sever the ties between man and sin. He loves people too much to allow them to continue in the sin that separates them from Him.

Jesus told him, "I am the way, the truth, and the life. No one comes to the Father except through me."

John 14:6

The most important truth of all is that no one can come to the Father except through Jesus. There is no other way. God uses believers to share their faith through encounters with people who need to hear that important truth. It is a matter of eternal life and death. We have been given an assignment by Jesus to tell others in Matthew 28:19-20, in what is called the Great Commission.

Scripture Readings

Hebrews 4:12
Psalm 119:160
Psalm 86:11
Matthew 22:16
John 8:31-32

Takeaway Questions

Do you recall a time when you realized your understanding of truth was false? If the answer is yes, note how accepting the truth of the Bible altered your worldview.

People are deceived by Satan's lies. How can you have encounters with others, during which you can counter those lies with biblical truth?

Deception is even coming from the pulpits of some modern churches. Unfortunately, many Christians are accepting that deception because they do not know better. How can you know for sure what is truth and what is not?

Notes

21

The Disciples' Foot-Washing Encounter

Encounter with Humility

JOHN 13

When artists attempt to recreate a likeness of a master, they use the original as a model. Christians are to emulate and model themselves on Jesus, the author and finisher of our faith. Jesus humbled Himself when He left heaven, came to earth, and lived a perfect sinless life. There never has been a greater demonstration of humility than the incarnation of Jesus. There is much written in the Bible that teaches us about the need for humility. Scripture describes humility as meekness, lowliness, and

Humility is the ability to be without pride or arrogance and it is a main character that should be seen in those who follow Jesus Christ. Jesus is the best example of someone who humbly followed God's plan for His life.

absence of self. The Greek word translated "humility" literally means lowliness of mind. Humility is a heart attitude, not merely an outward demeanor.

The Encounter

In John 13, Jesus' disciples encountered an experience that taught them much about humility. Their encounter was with each other and was used by Jesus as a teaching moment. This encounter took place at the Last Supper, just before the beginning of the Passover. It was a time when Jesus was fully aware His time on earth, and with the disciples He loved, was nearing an end. He got up from the supper and poured water into a basin and began to wash His disciples' feet and to dry them with the towel. When Jesus had washed their feet, He asked them if they understood what He had done for them. The disciples had previously called Him Master and Lord. Peter even proclaimed He was the long-anticipated Messiah. This same Jesus was willing to humble Himself and wash their feet as an example for them to be humble enough to wash each other's feet. His example for them is also an example for all Christians to follow. They had been taught a powerful lesson that evening as they experienced an encounter with humility.

A Life Application

My husband loves to tell of when he was a deacon several years ago, in a church in Florida. Each year one of the monthly deacons' meetings was dedicated to the deacons washing each other's feet. The deacon ministry was established in Acts 6, where deacons were to be servants ministering to widows and orphans. In the church my husband attended, their title was servant-deacons. My husband says it was one of the most moving and humbling experiences of his life. He looked forward to it each year as a reminder to always remain humble. Each encounter we have with humility is a lesson in what is important in the Christian life. Humility and pride cannot co-exist in the same person.

When Jesus delivered the Sermon on the Mount, He said, **"Blessed are the humble for they will inherit the earth"** (Mt. 5:5). He taught that any person who wants to be the greatest must portray him or herself as the least. Humility was a theme in much of what Jesus taught His disciples.

> **12 Whoever exalts himself will be humbled, and whoever humbles himself will be exalted.**
>
> Matthew 23:12

Humility is a primary characteristic of Spirit-filled people. The Apostle Paul in his letter to the Philippian church wrote about humility.

> **3 Do nothing out of selfish ambition or conceit, but in humility consider others as more important than yourselves. 4 Everyone should look not to his own interests, but rather to the interests of others.**
>
> Philippians 2:3-4

In verses 5 through 11, he described the greatest example of humility was Jesus, who left heaven, emptied Himself and became as humble as a servant. When Paul used the term "emptied Himself," he defined humility. To be humble is to empty oneself of ego and pride.

Scripture teaches that everything should be done with humility, not out of selfish ambition or conceit. It is to consider others as more important than ourselves. In other words, a humble person looks not to his own interests, but rather to the interests of others.

Calls for humility are not limited to the New Testament. In 2 Chronicles there is a call for God's people to humble themselves and turn from their ungodly ways. It was a prerequisite for God to forgive His people and to heal their land. The message is for God's people, not those who do not belong to Him.

Biblical humility is being comfortable with who we are in Christ and seeking to build up others rather than ourselves. It involves confidence that God is is in control and we are His vessel on earth.

Jesus treated the lowest segment of society with dignity and respect. In doing so, He showed compassion for others, and even dined with tax collectors and others despised by the prevalent culture. The Bible details the lives of many others who were humble. To name a few: Moses, Joseph, Paul, David, Ruth, and even Mary, the mother of Jesus. Scripture tells us God does not forget the cry of the humble, the meek (humble) will inherit the earth, and there is wisdom with the humble.

In Matthew 20, there is the story of a lack of humility when the mother of James and John asked Jesus to allow her sons to sit next to Him in heaven. He explained to her that only the Father could grant her request. The other apostles became indignant when they heard of her request. Jesus responded by teaching them an important lesson on humility.

> *"26 It must not be like that among you. On the contrary, whoever wants to become great among you must be your servant, 27 and whoever wants to be first among you must be your slave; 28 just as the Son of Man did not come to be served, but to serve, and to give his life as a ransom for many."*
>
> Matthew 20:26-28

As Christians read what the Bible says about humility, they should reassess their own humility. Are we humble or do we struggle with pride? Followers of Christ must take the calling for humility seriously and not possess a haughty and prideful spirit. James 4:6, 10 aptly discusses pride and humility.

> *6 God resists the proud but gives grace to the humble.*

> ***10** Humble yourselves before the Lord, and he will exalt you.*

Knowing all blessings come from God should be humbling for us. Everything we have has been provided by the Lord. Truly thankful people have frequent encounters with humility as they fall on their faces and prayerfully tell God they are sorry for their pride and arrogance. Jesus treated the people He encountered with respect and dignity because, while He was still God, He also was a humble and thankful man. Be encouraged to live out your life with the attitude that you are humbled to be a Christian. Modern culture has been built on pride. Christian culture should be built on humility. Christians should experience an encounter with humility each day.

> *Forgive us, oh Lord for our arrogance and lack of humility. You and You alone are to be exalted.*

Scripture Reading

John 13
Matthew 5
Galatians 5:22-23
Philippians 22
Chronicles 7:14

Takeaway Questions

Did reading about the Bible's call for humbleness make you consider your own spirit? Do you have more pride in your life than an attitude of humility? Make notes.

How can you reshape your thinking to become a humbler person?

Why do you think Jesus placed so much emphasis on the need for believers to be humble?

Notes

22

Josiah's Encounter with The Book of God

King Josiah Encounters God's Holy Book

2 Chronicles 24

Can you imagine a world without the Word of God? That is exactly the world the Isaelities lived in for several centuries. Without God's Word, there is no truth or guide to righteous living. The Bible provides a plumb line for life, and without it there is only Satan's lies, sin, and evil. Becaue they did not have the truth of God's Word, the Israelites

"3 In the eighth year of his reign, while he was still a youth, Josiah began to seek the God of his ancestor David, and in the twelfth year he began to cleanse Judah and Jerusalem of the high places, the Asherah poles, the carved images, and the cast image"s.

2 Chronicles 34:3

resorted to worshipping false idols and gods. King Josiah changed all that when he found God's Holy Book.

The Encounter

Josiah was the sixteenth king of Judah (c. 640–609 BCE) who instituted major religious reforms. He became king of Judah at the age of eight, after the assassination of his father, King Amon. His reign lasted thirty-one years. Josiah's story can be found in 2 Chronicles 34 and 2 Kings 22. 2 Chronicles 34:2 says he did right in the the Lord's sight.

During his reign, Josiah ordered the removal of all semblence of false idols and the restoration of the Temple. He cleansed Judah and Jerusalem. Also during his reign, he ordered the repair of the Temple of the Lord. During those repairs, workers found the book of the law of the Lord, written by Moses. When Josiah heard the words of the law, he tore his clothes.

> *"For great is the Lord's wrath that is poured out on us because our ancestors have not kept the word of the Lord in order to do everything written in this book."*
> 2 Chronicles 34:21

The tearing of clothing was an expression of horror and grief in ancient Israel. Josiah's grief was for his nation. His was an expression of deep conviction of sin. Realizing the wrath that was due the people for not keeping God's law, he sought information from the prophetess Huldah. She reported the Lord said He would bring disaster on His people because they had abandoned Him and worshipped other gods. The Lord also had a personal message for Josiah.

> 27 "'...because your heart was tender and you humbled yourself before God when you heard his words against this place and against its inhabitants, and because you humbled yourself before me, and you tore your clothes and wept before me, I myself have heard'—this is the Lord's declaration. 28 'I will indeed gather you to your ancestors, and you will be gathered to your grave in peace. Your eyes will not see all the disaster that I am bringing on this place and on its inhabitants.'"
>
> 2 Chronicles 34:27-28

Josiah read all the words of the book of the law that had been found in the Lord's Temple. Then he made a covenant to follow the Lord and to keep His commands with all his heart and with all his soul to carry out the words of the covenant written in the book. Josiah removed everything detestable from all the lands belonging to the Israelites, and he required all who were present in Israel to serve the Lord their God. Throughout his reign, they did not turn aside from following the Lord, the God of their ancestors.

A Life Application

When Josiah had an encounter with God's Word, it changed everything for him. It is remarkable that God's Holy Word had been lost to His covenent people for centuries and they did not even miss it. Without God's Word to guide them, they had lapsed into doing evil. There was no way of knowing the heart of God, so they accepted false truths. Finding the book of the law gave Josiah an altogether new perspective. With it, he realized the people were destined to receive the wrath of God and it gave him a true perspective on how to live his own life and provide leadership for his people.

2 Chronicles 34 is a lesson as to what happens when people encounter God's Word. To please God there must be an ongoing encounter with His Word. It is necessary to be spiritually healthy.

> **25 The truly happy people are those who carefully study God's perfect law that makes people free, and they continue to study it. They do not forget what they heard, but they obey what God's teaching says.**
>
> James 1:25

We have not lost the Book of God, but the world is increasingly rejecting it. Without God's truth, everything is based on false information. Judges 21:25 describes a world absent of God's truth: every man did what was right in his own eyes. God's Word establishes a guide for life and forms the basis for all mankind to have an eternal relationship with their Creator. The Bible is the best-selling book of all time because man has an innate need to know God, and His Word fills that need. It has also inspired great discoveries, art, music, and has changed lives throughout the ages.

The Israelites lived their lives in disobedience to God's law because they did not have the knowledge to do otherwise. Many people have beliefs that are either based on lies or misinformation. To know what to belive requires a constant encounter with God's Word. Soaking up the truth is the only way to focus on right, not evil.

Josiah was a leader of his nation. Once he understood God's book, he was able to be a leader with spiritual insight. It would be wonderful if the leaders in our modern culture did the same. The world needs leaders who know God's Word and will use it as they lead others. The Bible commands Christians to pray for political leaders.

The Bible has the power to change lives because it is the living Word of God. We must actively seek to fill our hearts with God's Word each day. When we do these things, God changes our heart. When our heart is changed, our life is changed.

There may come a time when God's Word will be taken away. When scripture is memorized and engraved on people's hearts, it cannot be removed. We have a task to help people understand right from wrong. That is done by teaching them about the Bible. Modern culture does not consider God's Word as relevant. If that pattern persists, it will result in a society with no understanding or plumb line for righteous living. They will lose God's word and will not even miss it.

Scripture Reading

2 Chronicles 34
2 Kings 22

Takeaway Questions

What are your thoughts about a people who could lose the Word for God and never realize it? What do you believe our culture would look like if we did not have the Bible?

Do you have a regular encounter with God's Word? If the answer is no, note how you can improve that.

What can you do to help people understand the importance of the Bible?

Notes

23

The Disciples' Encounter with a Storm.

Encounters with Storms of Life

LUKE 8

*L*ife is full of storms. Storms may be physical events such as hurricanes, tornadoes, or floods, but often they come in the form of a death of a loved one, loss of income, divorce, or any other event that causes fear, pain, or anxiety.

The Encounter

The gospel writer Luke records the story of a physical storm that caused fear for some of Jesus' disciples. One day, Jesus and His disciples got into a boat and sailed to the east side of the Sea of Galilee. During the voyage, a huge storm arose, which was causing the boat to sink. The disciples were terrified, and Jesus, all the while, was comfortably asleep in the lower part of the ship. The frenzied disciples awoke Jesus with the words, "Master, Master, we are going to die." With simple words, Jesus calmed the winds and waves and all was once again calm. Of course, they were amazed and wondered who Jesus was that He could command the wind and waves.

A Life Application

Several years ago, my husband and I joined a group of fellow believers on a trip to Israel. I remember waking up one morning in a hotel room in Tiberias on the shore of the Sea of Galilee, as a tremendous storm raged across the lake. The wind howled down between the Golan Heights on the east side of the lake and the hills of Galilee to the west. I was amazed at how powerful those

"Then a fierce windstorm came down on the lake; they were being swamped and were in danger. They came and woke him up, saying, "Master, Master, we're going to die!" Then he got up and rebuked the wind and the raging waves. So they ceased, and there was a calm. He said to them, "Where is your faith?" They were fearful and amazed, asking one another, "Who then is this? He commands even the winds and the waves, and they obey him!"
Luke 8:23-25

winds were and how they totally turned the lake into a raging body of water. As I watched the storm, I could not help but think about the fear the disciples experienced on that fateful voyage. Then Jesus calmed the storm.

Life is never without trials, and everyone encounters storms as they live out their lives. It is as natural as day and night. The question is how we react to those inevitable storms. The Bible records many storms that affected people in both the Old and New Testaments. Job faced a storm when he lost everything he possessed, including his family. Jesus ended His Sermon on the Mount by telling His listeners that everyone who hears His words, and acts on them, is like a wise man who builds his house on rock rather than sand. When the storms come, the house will stand firm because it has been founded on the rock. Those who hear His words, and do not act on them, will be like a foolish man who builds his house on sand, which storms will inevitably destroy.

The Babylonians swept down upon and destroyed Jerusalem and the Temple in 597 B.C., and the residents were taken into Babylonian captivity. The Israelites experienced a terrible storm for the next seventy years. Prior to the destruction of Jerusalem, God gave a message (Jer. 29:11-13) to His prophet Jeremiah to be shared with the city's inhabitants. They would experience a storm like no other they had ever known, but God let them know He had plans for them, and those plans were not to harm them but to prosper them and to give them a hope and a future. God was in control of the events surrounding His people.

I mentioned earlier observing a violent storm rage over the Sea of Galilee. A few days later, I saw those same waters in a vastly different manner. It was a beautiful Mother's Day afternoon. My husband and I were sitting on a large rock on the side of the same mountain where Jesus spoke the Sermon on the Mount. The mountain is situated above the town of Capernaum and overlooks the Sea of Galilee. It was warm, the sun was shining, and a gentle breeze caused ripples on the water that dazzled in the sunlight. As I gazed over the tranquil waters of the lake, I listened as others read the words of Jesus spoken on that same mountainside two thousand years ago. The scene was calm, and His words were reassuring and hopeful. It was a time to savor the calm when there were no raging storms.

My two Sea of Galilee experiences are a reminder to me that God loves us while we are in the storms of life and lets us experience them so we will better appreciate the calm times. He loved His disciples when they were afraid of the storm, and He loved those who listened as He preached the Sermon on the Mount. It seems that sometimes we only learn lessons during our biggest storms.

Like all people, I have experienced troubling storms in my life. When I was in high school, I was riding on a school bus when the driver accidently closed the door on my little sister's foot, then ran over and killed her. Words cannot describe how devastating a storm the events of that day brought on me and my family. The storm never fully subsided for my parents. My life has never been the same since that day. I became determined that I would never experience pain like that again. To protect myself, I closed myself off to feelings. My reaction to a major storm in my life negatively impacted my relationships with others for many years. It took time, but I finally learned to trust in the one who calms the raging storms.

I also lived in the storm of a controlling and abusive marriage for thirty years. When the storm ended, I was able to understand that, like the captive Israelites in

Jeremiah's day, God had a plan for me. While the marriage was painful, it produced two wonderful children and I now can enjoy five beautiful granddaughters. I chose to appreciate that I survived the storm rather than allow it to continue to rage in my life. My faith and trust in Jesus calmed my personal storm. Over the years, I have known several people who have not overcome the storms that once impacted their lives. Sadly, by keeping their storms alive they miss out on the joy and happiness God wants for them. The disciples' fear turned to assurance when they called on Jesus to still the raging winds and water.

God eventually brought a wonderful man into my life who has been my helpmate for twenty-three years. He came with a beautiful daughter who has added so much love to our family. God has opened doors for me to share my experiences of living through a season of storms in my first marriage to counsel and mentor other

"Be gracious to me, God, be gracious to me, for I take refuge in you. I will seek refuge in the shadow of your wings until danger passes".
Psalms 51:1

women who are encountering their own storms of abusive relationships. I thank God that He prepared me for this ministry. I would be unable to help others weather their storms if I had not lived through my own. God did have a plan for my life, and it was for good and not harmful for me.

I have learned that age brings perspective to life. When in the middle of life's storms, we often expend far too much energy fighting against the raging waves. It can be much like a drowning swimmer. During the struggle to survive they exhaust all their energy and finally the waters claim them. Later in life, we can see how God was working through those storms and how His plans were infinitesimally better than anything we could have imagined. The energy wasted fighting the storms is saved when we place our trust in the Master of the seas.

Many people live in fear during the storms of life. The year 2020 was one of the most trying years that anyone can remember. A pandemic swept across the planet. There were more violent storms than any time in recorded history. American cities were plagued with riots and civil disturbances that turned social order into social disorder. On top of everything else, it was also an election year that was extremely disruptive. The news and social media constantly bombarded the world with troubling news throughout the year. The pandemic, social and physical storms, while they seem gigantic, are minimal compared to the spiritual storms that are raging throughout our culture. People without Christ have nothing to alleviate their fears. There is good news, however. God still reigns and is not surprised or unnerved by anything the year has offered. He still has the power to calm raging storms. The question we must ask ourselves is: Do we have faith sufficient to trust God to calm the storms that so readily surround us? With Jesus on our side, there is no need to live in fear.

> *Then He arose and rebuked the wind, and said to the sea, "Peace, be still!" And the wind ceased and there was a great calm.*

> **40 But He said to them, "Why are you so**
> **fearful? How is it that you have no faith?"**
> Mark 4:39-40

During all the recent upheaval and unheard-of storms, God has worked in miraculous ways. His church has embarked on new methods to reach a lost world through electronic and social media. The gospel is now being spread around the world as never before. The pandemic closed churches and Christians suddenly were awakened to the fact that church attendance is a precious gift that may not always be available. Christians have been stirred to a new urgency. Our sense of complacency is no longer permissible. No matter the storm, God is still calming troubled waters. A key to experiencing victory in the middle of life's storms is to trust in God for deliverance and to praise Him. The songwriter has penned "I will sing praise, I will lift my voice, I will sing praise, I've made my choice. I will sing praise in all I do. I will sing praise to you. **No matter the storms that come my way, No matter the trials I may face, You promised that you would see me through. So, I will trust in You."**

We have the advantage of knowing exactly who Jesus is and His power to overcome every storm of life. The Bible tells story after story of God intervening in the lives of His people to calm the storms of life. Do we trust in Him, or do we find ourselves, like the disciples in the boat, fearful? The answer for their fear was just waiting for them to ask for His help. He is still waiting for us to ask Him to calm the raging storms in our lives.

In 1880, British Minister Vernon J. Charlesworth wrote a beautiful hymn entitled, *A Shelter in a Time of Storm*. His words perfectly describe the shelter Jesus provides as we encounter the storms of life. Charlesworth wrote the Lord is a mighty rock, a shelter in the time of storm. The hymn goes on to relate many of life's storms and that Jesus is always ready to be our shelter.

Scripture Reading

Luke 8:22-25
Matthew 8:23-27
Mark 4:35-41

Takeaway Questions

Have you experienced stormy times in your life? Describe them. Did God calm down the angry waves? Note how you might have wasted energy trying to fix what God could easily do,

Most people tend to try to fix things using their own power. That is what our society teaches us to do. Why is it so hard to turn over life's problems to God and let Him handle them?

How can you use the lessons you learned during your storms in life to help others who are traveling through their own personal storms?

Notes

_____

_____

_____

_____

_____

_____

_____

_____

_____

_____

_____

_____

_____

_____

_____

_____

24

Three Men's
Encounter with Fire

Shadrach, Meshach, and Abednego Encounter a Fiery Furnace

DANIEL 3

*D*aniel 3 captures one of the greatest examples of unshakable faith in God that have been recorded in the Bible. The events described took place during the seventy-year period the Israelites were in Babylonian captivity. King Nebuchadnezzar believed himself to be above everyone else, including God, and did not have to answer to anyone.

The Encounter

The story begins with a plan conceived by King Nebuchadnezzar to build a gigantic gold statue. He then commanded that everyone must fall facedown and worship his gold statue. Anyone who refused to worship the statue was to be immediately thrown into a furnace of blazing fire. It was reported to Nebuchadnezzar that three Israelites, Shadrach, Meshach, and Abednego, would not worship the statue. In a furious rage, Nebuchadnezzar ordered that they be brought to him. He told them if they did not worship his statue, they would immediately be thrown into a fiery furnace. He further challenged their God. They responded to the king by saying if the God they served existed, then He could rescue them from the furnace and He could rescue them from the power of Nebuchadnezzar. But even if He did not rescue them, they wanted the king to know that they would not serve his gods or worship the statue.

They had three important encounters at that point. One was standing up to the powerful King Nebuchadnezzar. Another was an encounter with a test of their faith, and the third was an encounter with fire.

Nebuchadnezzar gave orders to heat the furnace seven times more than was customary and he ordered Shadrach, Meshach, and Abednego be tied up and thrown into the furnace When Nebuchadnezzar investigated the furnace, he saw four men, not three, walking around in the fire unharmed; and the fourth looked like a son of the gods. He called them to come out of the furnace. As they emerged from the fire, they exhibited no effect of the fire, not a hair of their heads was singed, their robes were unaffected, and there was not even a smell of fire on them.

Nebuchadnezzar was so amazed, he praised the God of Shadrach, Meshach, and Abednego. God had rescued

His servants who had placed their trust in Him. They violated the king's command and risked their lives rather than serve or worship any god except the God of Israel. He said there was no other god who could deliver like that of Shadrach, Meshach, and Abednego.

Daniel also experienced a similar test of faith when he was thrown into the lion's den. There are many other examples of the faith of God's people being tested. Some tests are more extreme than others, but they are tests nonetheless. When Shadrach, Meshach, and Abednego were tested, they showed their faith was unshakable.

"If the God we serve exists, then he can rescue us from the furnace of blazing fire, and he can rescue us from the power of you, the king. But even if he does not rescue us, we want you as king to know that we will not serve your gods or worship the gold statue you set up."
Daniel 3:17-18

A Life Application

It has been said that fear is the absence of trust. Faith in God involves trust and firm belief that He is able do anything He wishes. This story shows how God acted on behalf of Shadrach, Meshach, and Abednego and He was glorified as a result. They knew God might not rescue them, but that was okay. They accepted God's will regardless of how the outcome affected them.

Sometimes we base our faith on the belief that God will always answer our prayers the way we want them answered. That is not how God works. He has plans that are larger than our wants. The challenge is for us to survive the test of faith and still trust in Him. This story illustrates the need for God's people to boldly take a stand for our Savior. The idols people bow and pay umbrage to today are different. There are the idols of ego, money, prestige, convenience, lust, and pride. False prophets abound who proclaim that all roads lead to heaven and everything is permissible if it feels good. When people believe in these falsehoods and place their trust in them, they make them their idols. When people bow down and worship idols and false gods, they open the doors to the greatest fiery furnace of all, hell.

Like Shadrach, Meshach, and Abednego, God's people are increasingly faced with demands to worship false idols. Governments are increasingly enacting laws that are in direct conflict with God's law. Nebuchadnezzar believed he was bigger than God and made his own law, which tried to force three of God's faithful servants to worship a false god. They chose to worship the only true God and were willing to accept His will regardless of how it affected them. Are we willing to do as they did and stand on God's law when there can be dire consequences? We live in a time when there is an increasing chorus to silence those who proclaim the Bible as truth. Times like these were predicted by Jesus throughout His earthly ministry. We should not be surprised by the ever-increasing war against Christianity in the world today. Be assured, God has not been caught off guard. Shadrach. Meshach and Abednego were willing to serve God even if it meant that His ultimate plan might not have included saving them. We are challenged to trust God who walks through the fire with us.

This is another story of people who faced tremendous pressure to act in ways they knew to be contrary to the will of God. The events of the story may have occurred thousands of years ago, but God's people continue to live under the threat of fire. It may not be physical fire, but it is fire nonetheless. When faced with the pressure to talk and act in ways that conflict with our spiritual beliefs, we must refuse to bow. We must stand tall for our Savior regardless of the consequences. Shadrach, Meshach, and Abednego set the example for us to follow.

Scripture Reading

Daniel 3

Takeaway Questions

Have you experienced fiery times in your life when your faith was challenged? How did you respond to that?

What did you learn about Shadrach, Meshach, Abednego and God in this study? How can you use what you learned in your personal walk through life?

How can you use the lessons you learned during your personal tests of faith in life to help others who are traveling through their own personal times of fire?

Notes

25

Encounter with a Savior

An Encounter with Jesus

LUKE I

*T*he final encounter in this study is also the most important encounter in the history of the world. The world encountered a Savior when the Virgin Mary gave birth to Jesus.

The Encounter

The birth of the Messiah had been predicted by the Old Testament prophets for centuries. The writer Luke describes the fulfillment of those prophecies in chapter 1 of his gospel. An angel appeared to a virgin named Mary who was engaged to a man named Joseph, a descendant of David. The angel told Mary she would conceive and give birth to a son and name Him Jesus. Mary was told Jesus would be called the Son of God, who would give the child the throne of His father David and His kingdom would never end.

It was humanly impossible for Mary to understand all she had been told, so she told the angel she was a virgin and asked how she could become pregnant. The angel told her conception would come from God through the Holy Spirit. This news must have been earth-shattering for both Mary and Joseph. Though they did not comprehend all that had been revealed to them, they were obedient. Mary's encounter with the angel resulted in her hearing something that no other woman in history would ever hear. As a virgin, she would bring the long-anticipated Messiah into the world. The Prophet Isaiah had prophesied hundreds of years earlier that a virgin would conceive, and the son to be born would be named Immanuel, God with us. The Prophet Micah wrote the Messiah would be born in Bethlehem.

"Therefore, the Lord himself will give you a sign: The virgin will conceive and give birth to a son, and will call him Immanuel."
Isaiah 7:14

"But you, Bethlehem Ephrathah, though you are small among the clans of Judah, out of you will come for me one who will be ruler over Israel, whose origins are from of old, from ancient times."
Micah 5:2.

Two thousand years later, people still cannot accept the truth of the virgin birth of Jesus. God is bigger than what people are willing to believe.

A Life Application

When Jesus was born, the world experienced an encounter with a Savior. A Savior who was both the complete God and a perfect man. No other man has ever lived or ever will live who has His perfect, unblemished nature. With the birth of Jesus, the world was given a perfect sinless sacrifice to take on the sin nature that had entered man with Adam's fall. Adam was the head of Old Creation (Gen. 1:26) and Christ became the head of the New Creation.

The world has been dominated by sin since Adam's fall in the Garden of Eden. Adam was made perfect by God but lost his perfection when he disobeyed God. From Adam, mankind inherited sin and its wages, which is eternal death (Rom. 5:12; 6:23). Sin separates all mankind from their Creator. God wants to have a relationship with mankind but is unable to do so when man continues in sin. Only Jesus could bridge that gap—and He did. God's plan always included the incarnation of His Son Jesus to be the Savior the world desperately needed.

When the world encountered Jesus, it was the most remarkable encounter that would ever occur in human history. Normal encounters are between two human beings. However, the birth of Jesus was a physical encounter between God and His created mankind. It was an encounter in which God became man and spent thirty-three years living among mankind, during which He experienced everything that all people experience, except sin. Those experiences included the highest level of evil when His fellow man brought about His crucifixion. His physical encounter with man included pain and death to save mankind from the evil that destroys them. On the cross, Jesus took the punishment that all mankind deserved for sin. He did not deserve to die, but He willingly took mankind's place and experienced death to take on the penalty of sin.

The Jews had long been expecting a Messiah who would come as a powerful king to rid them of the dreaded Romans. The birth of the Messiah was not what they wanted or expected, so they rejected Him. Their rejection opened the door for all people to have access to God and to be saved from their sin. They made a fateful choice, to continue in religion and reject a relationship with God. People continue today to choose their present lifestyles over a relationship with their maker. As we explore the incarnation of Jesus, it is important to understand some key points about His birth and ministry. When Mary gave birth to Jesus, it was not the beginning of the Son of God. He has always existed as part of the Trinity of God. When man was created, Jesus was there.

> **26. Then God said, "Let us make mankind in our image, in our likeness, so that they may rule over the fish in the sea and the birds in the sky, over the livestock and all**

> *the wild animals, and over all the creatures*
> *that move along the ground."*
>
> Genesis 1:26

While Jesus had always existed, His birth marked His physical entry into the world and becoming one of us. His birth also shows His humility. Jesus was not the type of king the Jews were expecting. He came as a humble man, starting with His birth in a stable.

> *5 Adopt the same attitude as that of Christ Jesus, 6 who, existing in the form of God, did not consider equality with God as something to be exploited. 7 Instead he emptied himself by assuming the form of a servant, taking on the likeness of humanity. And when he had come as a man, 8 he humbled himself by becoming obedient to the point of death—even to death on a cross.*
>
> Philippians 2:5–8

His birth had been predicted in the Old Testament and was in accordance with God's eternal plan.

> *6 For a child will be born for us, a son will be given to us, and the government will be on his shoulders. He will be named Wonderful Counselor, Mighty God, Eternal Father, Prince of Peace.*
>
> Isaiah 9:6

Most importantly, the birth of Jesus was necessary for man's salvation. His birth, death and resurrection were required for mankind to have an eternal relationship with their Creator. The writer of Hebrews wrote:

> *17. Therefore, he had to be like his brothers and sisters in every way, so that he could become a merciful and faithful high priest in matters pertaining to God, to make atonement^J for the sins of the people.*
>
> Hebrews 2:17

When Jesus left His home in heaven, He became homeless on earth. I once heard it said that all Christians are homeless since our home is in heaven. That is an interesting concept to grasp. There is a tendency to become so comfortable on earth that Christians lose sight of where their home really is. Jesus was on earth, but His Father was in heaven. The same is true of believers today: our Father is in Heaven. Jesus gave up everything in heaven to save mankind from the grip of Satan.

The Bible records many references that confirm that Jesus is the Savior of the world.

> *14 And we have seen and testify that the Father has sent his Son to be the Savior of the world.*
>
> 1 John 4:14

"Today in the town of David a Savior has been born to you; he is the Messiah, the LORD."

Luke 2:11

They said to the woman, "We no longer believe just because of what you said; now we have heard for ourselves, and we know that this man really is the Savior of the world."

John 4:42

In 1719, a Methodist minister named Isaac Watts penned a hymn based on Psalm 98, Psalm 96, and Genesis 3. It is known as the Christmas carol, *Joy to the World*. It became the most-published Christmas hymn in North America. Watts's lyrics declare the Lord has come to the earth and brought joy as He reigns as Savior. Heaven and nature sing at the wonders of His love.

The most wonderful news ever to be recorded is that the birth of Jesus truly did bring joy to the world because it brought a Savior to a lost and dying world. There is no greater joy than being safely held in the arms of the Savior. That Savior is still available to redeem lost and dying people. Christians have the responsibility to tell the world of the hope and joy that only Jesus can provide. The world has never been in greater need of an encounter with a Savior. The world has had an encounter with a Savior and the unfortunate thing is that most people do not even know they need a Savior, or they choose to reject Him. Man does need a Savior, and God has provided one. Jesus demonstrates God's love and His mercy

> *"16 For God loved the world in this way: He gave his one and only Son, so that everyone who believes in him will not perish but have eternal life. 17 For God did not send his Son into the world to condemn the world, but to save the world through him. 18 Anyone who believes in him is not condemned, but anyone who does not believe is already condemned, because he has not believed in the name of the one and only Son of God."*
>
> John 3:16-18

The Savior Himself gave us a command to tell the world they need an encounter with their only hope of redemption. The consequences of people not accepting the Savior go well beyond this world, they are eternal. That is a sobering thought. It should motivate us to understand the urgency of being more focused and intentional in all our encounters. The eternity of people's souls depends on it. It is my prayer that your encounters with others will be the most important ones they will ever experience. It is an encounter with eternal implications. John Wesley once said, "Let us Go, tell it on the mountain, over the hills and everywhere; go, tell it on the mountain that Jesus Christ is born."

Scripture Reading

Isaiah 7:14
Isaiah 53:5
Micah 5:2
Matthew 2:1-12
Luke 1:39-45
John 3:16
Acts 10:43
Timothy 1:15

Takeaway Questions

How often do you stop and meditate on the encounter the earth had with its Savior? Stop and examine the deep meaning of the encounter,

Do you make it your mission to encounter others with the good news of the Savior? How?

What is your perception of the world if Jesus had not come to save mankind from their sins?

Notes

Postscript

The encounters detailed in this book may have occurred several thousand years ago, but the lessons to be learned from them are as eternal as the Bible itself. A key question one should always ask when reading scripture is: What can I learn from this to live my life in the twenty-first century? What encounters in your life have redirected you? What encounters will God present you with in the future, and how will you react? You might be someone else's encounter that changes their life.

I was inspired to write about these encounters because they all are more than simple encounters, they are divine appointments that are examples for us to use as we live out our Christian lives in a modern world. While the stories are brief, I believe they can inspire modern readers as they approach everyday encounters. The encounters described were divine appointments that changed lives at the time they occurred and have continued to do so for many centuries. Another motivation was for the reader to take time to delve into God's Word, study it, meditate on it, and share it.

Reading of these encounters needs to be more than recounting ancient biblical history. These encounters should inspire us to consider the eternal importance of our encounters. Every encounter does indeed matter. Each Christian has had an encounter with another person who helped them to ultimately place their faith in Christ. That's the way it is with encounters: they are opportunities God has placed in people's lives. It is up to the participants in the encounters to make use of what God has orchestrated. Take every encounter as a possible divine appointment.

About the Author

$\mathcal{S}$ ue Z McGray is a Christian author, speaker, blogger and businesswoman. Sue was raised in rural Middle Tennessee by Christian parents who taught biblical values to their family. Even with that background, Sue unfortunately grew up with the misguided belief that her acceptance was based on personal performance. She felt she was never good enough, smart enough, or could do enough to earn love and respect. As a result, she became a people pleaser and suffered from co-dependence. Her self-esteem was so low, she felt invisible.

Sue overcame her early adversity to become a phenomenally successful businesswoman with an international cosmetics company. Her product was cosmetics, but her mission has always been encouraging women through intentional encounters. Her desire is to teach others that it is never too late for hope.

Sue has served as a regional director for the Christian Women in Media Association and presently serves as a member of their advisory board. For several years, Sue served as a member of the Board of Directors for Morning Star Shelter, a Christian organization that provides refuge, encouragement, and training for victims of domestic violence and their children. She continues to serve as a mentor to women recovering from crisis.

Sue is an ambassador for The Mary Kay Foundation, a charitable foundation that supports cancer research and domestic violence recovery and assistance.

She is the author of **Becoming Visible, Letting Go of the Things that Hide Your True Beauty,** and has been a contributor for other authors in their works. She is a frequent guest on faith-based podcasts, television, and radio programs, is a public speaker and a blogger.

Sue is married to Duane and together they have three children and five granddaughters.

If you enjoyed this book, please tell others…

- Write about Life-*Changing Encounters and Divine Appointments* on your blog, Twitter, Facebook and your other social medial sites.
- Suggest *Life-Changing Encounters and Divine Appointments* to friends.
- This book is available through all major distributors. If your bookstore does not have *Life-Changing Encounters and Divine Appointments*, ask if they will order it for you.
- Write a positive review of *Life-Changing Encounters and Divine Appointments* on *www.amazon.com*.
- Purchase additional copies for gifts and Bible studies.

Connect with me:

www.suezmcgray.com
suez@suezmcgray.com
Facebook
LinkedIn
Twitter